UNVEILING THE GREEN

UNVEILING THE GREEN
Working Astrologically, Alchemically, and Psychologically with Plants

Sian Sibley

AEON

First edition published in 2022 by Black Lodge Publishing
This second edition published in 2025 by Aeon Books

Copyright © 2022, 2025 by Sian Sibley

The right of Sian Sibley to be identified as the author of this work has been asserted in accordance with §§ 77 and 78 of the Copyright Design and Patents Act 1988.

All rights reserved. No part of this publication may be reproduced, stored in a retrieval system, or transmitted, in any form or by any means, electronic, mechanical, photocopying, recording, or otherwise, without the prior written permission of the publisher.

British Library Cataloguing in Publication Data

A C.I.P. for this book is available from the British Library

ISBN-13: 978-1-80152-199-4

Typeset by Medlar Publishing Solutions Pvt Ltd, India

www.aeonbooks.co.uk

DEDICATION & THANKS

*This book is dedicated to Rowan and Joe who opened the door
and set me on my path.*

To my **Dragons** *both past and present, and to all those who dedicate
their time to the Craft, I thank you for the work, the fun, and always
pushing me to be more.*

*And not least to my other half—Wayne, thank you so much for
putting up with the crazy and for letting me just be Me!*

CONTENTS

FOREWORD TO THE SECOND EDITION — ix

INTRODUCTION — xiii

PART ONE: GENESIS

CHAPTER ONE
Beginnings — 3

CHAPTER TWO
The biology of the green — 11

CHAPTER THREE
Tackling your world view — 31

PART TWO: THE WORK

CHAPTER FOUR
The growing — 43

CHAPTER FIVE
Getting to know you… 53

CHAPTER SIX
Simple alchemical praxis 63

CHAPTER SEVEN
Making your practice magical 71

PART THREE: THE PLANTS

ILLUSTRATIONS & COMMENTARIES
    Mugwort 79
    Yew 89
    Poppy 101
    Monkshood 111
    Rosemary 117
    Marshmallow 125
    Buttercup 133
    Elder 139
    Bramble 149
    Lungwort 155
    Eyebright 165
    Columbine 173

CONCLUSION 179

BIBLIOGRAPHY 183

FOREWORD TO THE SECOND EDITION

When I first wrote *Unveiling the Green*, I was deeply immersed in the scientific aspects of plant spirits, their chemistry, their biology, and their intricate relationships with the world around them. I approached the subject with the precision of a scientist, laying out observations, mechanisms, and structured processes as though I were writing a laboratory manual. But, as time passed, and I gained more experience, not just as an author but as a practitioner, I realised that something was missing. The heart. The passion. The very essence of what makes our connection with the Green World so vital and transformative.

Writing three books has given me the perspective to see where I had held myself back, where I had let the language of science overshadow the deeper, more instinctual knowing that drives this work. Make no mistake, the science is important, and it's still in this book. I have always been someone who believes that knowledge, in all its forms, strengthens our practice. But, when it comes to plant spirits, to the soul of the Green, science alone does not tell the whole story.

This revision is not just an update to include the plants that I have been working with since writing this book; it is a reimagining. It is an invitation to walk with them, to listen, to learn, and, ultimately, to heal. Not just ourselves, but the world around us. And make no mistake, the world needs healing. We are living in a time when environmental destruction is not just happening, it is being actively encouraged. Right-wing governments, backed by corporate interests, are pushing a "humans first" agenda as though we are somehow separate from the ecosystems that sustain us. Policies are being rolled back, regulations gutted, all in the name of economic growth that benefits only the very few at the top.

And perhaps the most insidious part of it all is the way in which language is being twisted to manipulate public perception. Oil is being rebranded, and green energy vilified. Instead of acknowledging the catastrophic effects of fossil fuels, we are being fed a narrative that renewable energy is inefficient, unreliable, and even dangerous. The people in power are not just resisting the shift to sustainability; they are actively working to demonise it.

Take, for example, the resurgence of oil companies marketing themselves as "clean" and "necessary for stability". There is a deliberate effort to paint fossil fuels as the backbone of civilisation, while wind and solar energy are framed as weak, unstable, and somehow a threat to our way of life. It's not just misinformation, it's psychological warfare, designed to keep people dependent on systems that are poisoning the planet.

And then there are the absurd, almost cartoonish displays of arrogance, like the former and now sadly current US president bringing back plastic straws and mocking environmental concerns with a smirking "sorry, Mr. Shark". These moments are not just ignorance, they are calculated. They send a message that caring for the planet is something to be ridiculed, that environmentalists are hysterical and that the destruction of ecosystems is not just necessary but desirable. And people believe it. Because it is easier, isn't it? It is easier to keep drinking from plastic cups, to keep filling our cars with petrol, to keep living as though the world is infinite and indestructible. The alternative, the reality, is harder to face. It requires change. It requires accountability. And for those in power, it requires them to relinquish control over the systems that keep them rich.

This is where our work becomes vital. This is why this book matters. Because—when we connect with the Green World, truly connect, not just in an intellectual sense but in a deep, spiritual way—those illusions begin to fall apart. When we sit with a tree, when we listen to the whispers of leaves in the wind, when we experience firsthand the presence and wisdom of plant spirits, we remember something that has been buried under decades of propaganda and industrial expansion: we are not separate from nature, we are part of it. And what we do to the Earth, we do to ourselves. This is why the knowledge in this book is so important. Plant spirits are not just passive entities; they are allies, guides, and teachers. They offer us insight, healing, and, perhaps most importantly, a pathway back to a way of living that is in harmony with the natural world rather than at war with it. And yet, even within spiritual circles, this kind of connection is often dismissed. There is still a tendency to see plants as tools rather than beings, to approach herbalism and plant magic with a mindset that is extractive rather than reciprocal. But if we are to make real change, if we are to counteract the destruction that is being inflicted upon the Earth, we must go deeper.

This book is my attempt to help facilitate that depth. To move beyond the sterile, scientific descriptions, and instead weave something that is alive, something that breathes with the same energy as the forests, the fields, and the sacred groves.

It is easy to feel helpless in the face of what is happening in the world. When governments refuse to act, when corporations hold all the power, when the people trying to make a difference are silenced, it can feel as though there is nothing left to do but watch. But that is a lie. Change does not always come in sweeping political revolutions. More often, it happens in small, quiet moments. A seed planted. A tree protected. A person who chooses to live differently, who chooses to listen rather than take. And that is where our power lies. By engaging with plant spirits, by learning from them and working with them, we are not just practising an ancient and beautiful form of magic, we are participating in a radical act of resistance. We are choosing connection over consumption, reverence over exploitation. And that choice matters. If enough people make it, if enough people step away from the narrative that tells us we are separate, that nature is a resource rather than a kin, that the destruction of the planet is inevitable, then we can shift the tide one person at a time, one plant at a time.

This is why I have rewritten this book in a way that is less "sciencey" and more accessible. Because this knowledge should not be locked away in academic language or dry methodology. It should be something that speaks to people, something that feels alive and immediate. The wisdom of plant spirits is not just for scholars or seasoned practitioners; it is for everyone.

And if this book can help even one more person find their way back to the Green, then it will have done its job. Because the Earth needs us. The plants are waiting. And the time for action is now.

Let's walk this path together.

Sian Sibley

INTRODUCTION

By picking up this book, you've already proven something important: you believe that we're not the only beings on this planet that matter. That, my friend, makes you a radical. A subversive. Someone who stands apart from the mainstream of the western world. And that's a good thing. This book is here to help you move away from the narrow, human-centred way of seeing things, a mindset that's been the dominant reality for over 300 years.

Since the Industrial Revolution, the natural world has been treated as something to be used and exploited, a commodity with a price tag rather than a living, breathing entity. Everything—plants, animals, even people—gets assigned a value based on how useful it is, and once it's served its purpose, it's discarded. This is not just unsustainable and immoral, but it's also devastating to our mental health and our understanding of ecology. It rips us away from the truth of our existence—we are meant to be part of the living system of the Earth, not parasites feeding on it. And yet here we are, trapped in a machine that grinds us down in the name of profit. Consumerism has disconnected so many from the living web of this world, turning us into something closer to a virus than a conscious species. We invade, replicate, and destroy. In doing so, we become less and less alive in the truest sense of the word.

So, what's the way forward? My hope is that this book will help shift your perspective and, more importantly, your actions. As people shaped by a westernised worldview, we need to find our way back to our Green neighbours: plants, trees, spores, fungi, the real elders of this planet. They were here long before us and will be here long after. If we listen, they will teach us how to reconnect with the Earth's own consciousness and, ultimately, our place within it.

My journey started in the world of traditional magic and witchcraft. I had a relationship with plants, but back then they were offerings, sacrifices to the spirits and deities I worked with. They were correspondences in my magical work, tied to planets, spirits, and angels. I never truly saw them for what they were—beings in their own right.

That changed after a conversation with the author Gary Nottingham. We were talking about Alchemy (a shared passion) when we touched on the work of Charubel, a Welsh mystic who worked with the spirits of plants, not as physical medicines, but psychically. That conversation planted a seed in my mind, and soon after I had my first real encounter with Mugwort. The timing was too perfect to be a coincidence. That moment cracked the door open, and I stepped through into a deeper, more profound relationship with the plant world. That doorway has remained open ever since, leading me not only to new magical praxes, but to a fundamental shift in how I perceive the Divine.

By the time you finish this book, I hope you'll have the tools to form your own connection with the Green. You'll learn the meditative and psychic practices that will allow you to truly meet the plants as they are, not just as ingredients or correspondences. You'll explore alchemical praxis and astrological connections, learning how to create medicines, gateway tinctures, and plant sigils that align with your own practice. These are paths to deeper experimentation, a way to weave yourself back into the natural matrix of the kosmos.

But let's be clear, this book won't do the work for you. That's on you. Reading it is not enough. Your results will be YOUR results. They might be similar to mine, or they might be completely different, and that's exactly how it should be. In science, variation is often seen as a mistake, an error that invalidates the experiment. In magic, variation is proof that the work is real.

Your connection with our plant allies is personal, evolving, and unique to you. So please, don't treat this book like a rigid instruction manual—no grimoire should be. If your practice ends up being an exact replica of mine, then you've missed the point. This book is meant to guide, not dictate. Take what resonates; experiment and forge your own path. That's where the real magic lies.

PART ONE

GENESIS

CHAPTER ONE

Beginnings

When I set out to write this guide, my aim was simple: to share what I've learned from working with the *Green People*—those steadfast, leafy allies who have been part of my magical practice for years. I wanted to offer clear guidance for those looking to step onto this path themselves, helping them navigate the process of "unveiling the Green" with both purpose and practicality. At its core, this was always going to be a grimoire, a proper magical textbook rather than just musings on the joys of wandering through the undergrowth (though that's certainly a perk). The focus was threefold:

> Why this work matters—because understanding the "why" gives meaning to the practice.
> How to do it—because knowing where to start makes all the difference.
> How to get real results with specific plants—because magic, like gardening, works best when it's practical.

The second of these—how to actually do the work—was always going to take centre stage. This section would follow the structure of a traditional grimoire, laying out methods, insights, and hands-on practice. Think of it as less of a rulebook and more of a field guide, one that invites you to step into the Green World with confidence, curiosity, and maybe a bit of dirt under your fingernails.

However, as my work unfurled, it stirred and shifted, breathing with a life of its own, less a creation and more a reflection, a weaving of memory and truth. It became a map, tracing where, how, and when the rift between us and the wild first cracked open, marking the quiet unravelling of our bond with the land. And yet, within these threads, a whisper of renewal lingers; a beginning, an outstretched hand beckoning us beyond the confines of what we were taught. An invitation to pause, to listen, and to step forward into a different way of seeing, of knowing, and of being.

Through this, I offer a space to pause, to trace the tangled roots of how deeply embedded social, economic, religious, and philosophical threads have woven us into the ecological crisis we now face. But this isn't just a reckoning with the past, it's a call to think differently, to stir the embers of forgotten magic and rekindle our understanding of the world. It is an invitation to learn, to listen, and to remember what it means to walk alongside the Green, rather than apart from it.

Yet, to step into a new beginning, we must first understand the path ahead. And for that we turn to the foundations, the quiet architects of life itself. Every ecosystem finds its roots in the Green; they are the weavers, the breath-givers, the silent keepers of balance. Without them, nothing thrives. So we begin here, at the source, where the story of life unfolds in leaf and stem, in root and whisper.

Playing games in the biology classroom ...

One of my favourite questions to ask—whether in my biology classes or during my esoteric talks—is this: "Can you name a single food that isn't made by the Sun?" It's a deceptively simple question, yet more often than not it completely stumps people. Most have never really considered just how fundamental the Sun is to all life on Earth. We've been taught to think of it as just another part of the mechanical universe, a giant ball of burning gas floating in space, something distant and separate from us. But that couldn't be further from the truth.

When students do try to answer, they usually offer something like "Milk?" And that's when I step in and say, "Milk comes from cows,

cows eat plants, plants eat sunlight". You can try it with any food you like, it all leads back to the Sun.

What we so often fail to realise is that we are *light walkers*, living manifestations of the Sun's energy, shaped and sustained by its warmth. And our greatest allies in this are the green plants, the original alchemists, the ones who turn sunlight into life. They are the bridge between energy and existence, the reason we are here at all.

Stefano Mancuso, in his book *Brilliant Green*, describes our relationship with plants as one of "absolute, primordial dependence".[1] They make up ninety-nine percent of all life on Earth, while animal life, us included, barely scrapes together one percent. And yet, despite this staggering imbalance, we move through the world barely noticing them, treating them as background scenery, as objects to be used, consumed, profited from. We have forgotten to see them for what they truly are, beings of great intelligence, resilience, and wisdom, shaping the world long before we arrived and, most likely, long after we are gone.

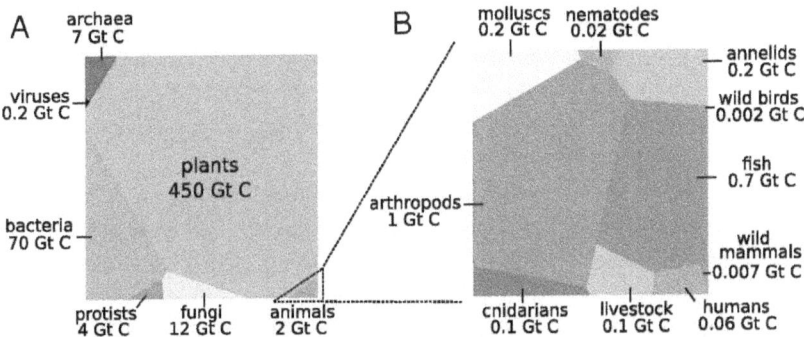

Figure 1. This graph shows the Biomass percentage population of the Earth (cf. Yinan Barr, Rob Phillips, and Ron Milo, June 2019 vol.115).

The truth about the dominant form of life on Earth is that it is definitely not us! We are late to the game, and when I say late, I mean wow, we are really late compared to the plants.

In the *Deep Green* project, a genetic analysis looking for the Eve species of plants, it was discovered that the earliest non-flowering plant was a tropical shrub called *Amborella*, which appeared around

---

[1] Stefano Mancuso and Alessandra Viola, *Brilliant green: the surprising history and science of plant intelligence* (Island Press, 2015).

135 million years ago. When we compare this plant's arrival to the latest figures for the existence of Homo sapiens (us), the evidence is of a paltry 150,000 years of species existence.

Try this to understand what I mean

Stand up and stretch your arms out as wide as they'll go, reaching from one side to the other. Now, imagine the entire evolutionary timeline laid out along this span—your arms forming a living, breathing chronology of life itself. Picture it like a massive index bar, where each point along your outstretched limbs marks a moment in Earth's history. Here's how it works ...

> i) From the right fingertip to the right shoulder—*No life (far too hot)*
> ii) From the right shoulder to the middle of the head—*Bacterial life/single celled plant life* and from which point *Plant life migrates to the land*
> iii) From the middle of the head to the left shoulder—*Single-celled animal life in the sea appears/Non-flowering plants established on the land*
> iv) From the left shoulder to left elbow—*Flowering plants on the land and fish in the sea begin to appear*
> v) From the elbow to mid-way through the forearm—*Trees and flowers are fully established/Amphibious life on the land will emerge*
> vi) From the mid-forearm to the wrist—*There are huge rain forests and wide plains/Reptiles and dinosaurs will appear*
> vii) From the wrist to the palm—*Plant life is well established and flourishing/Small mammalian life will appear*
> viii) From the palm to the middle finger knuckle—*The appearance of larger mammalian species*
> ix) From the knuckle to the nail—*This is where the first Hominid life appears.*
> x) From the cuticle of the nail to the end of the nail—*Homo sapiens, namely us, emerges*

This timeline gives you a visual way to grasp just how long plant life has been around, especially when you compare it to how late our own species showed up. So take a moment to really let that sink in and picture it in your mind's eye.

Plant blindness

One of the most incredible things about our plant friends is their ability to "hide" from us: that is, when they need to. We, as a race, are "plant blind". This is because plants have ALWAYS been here, and there has never been a version of the Earth that has not included plants. Plus, our greatest self-made stumbling block is that we perceive OURSELVES as sitting smugly at the pinnacle of the evolutionary pyramid.

For example, look at the image below and see if you can spot any plants:

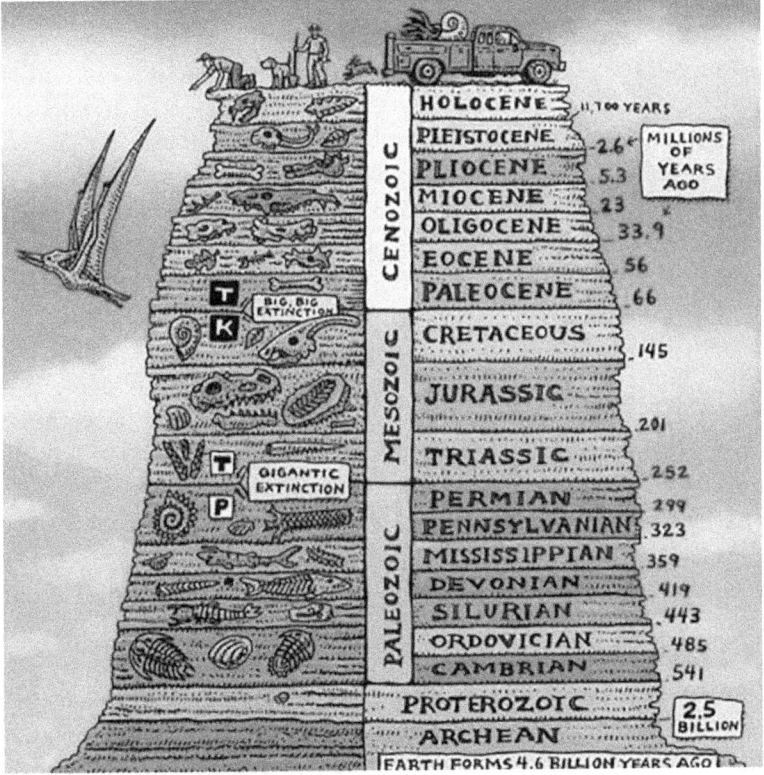

Well ... no, you can't spot them! Because even evolutionary science sometimes just ignores the plants.

Our gaze is drawn, time and again, to animals—especially ourselves—while plants fade into the background, overlooked, forgotten. Look to any chart of life, any model of existence, and the problem is laid bare: humans stand at the pinnacle, the centre of the story, while everything else is reduced to an afterthought, or worse, erased entirely. This is the heart of our disconnect. If we are ever to restore balance, we must unravel this old, flawed narrative and reweave our understanding. We must shift not only how we think but how we move through the world, recognising plants as kin, as living beings with their own intrinsic worth, not mere resources to be taken, used, and cast aside.

Before the Industrial Revolution, our relationship with plants was one of cooperation, a mutual exchange. We ate them, fed them to our livestock, and in return we, along with the animals, fertilised the land, spreading seeds both deliberately and unintentionally. We selected and replanted the crops that would sustain us through the seasons, ensuring that both we and the land flourished together. It was an interwoven existence; if the plants failed, so did we. Famine, hunger, and hardship were not abstract threats but immediate consequences of imbalance.

Plants were more than just food; they were medicine, healers, and allies. Even now, despite all our pharmaceutical advancements, nearly every modern medicine still owes its origins to the Green World. But the way we engage with plants has changed. Over centuries we have lost something vital: our intimacy with the land, our role as caretakers, our understanding that we are not separate from nature but deeply enmeshed within it.

This knowledge we once held was not just about science; it was instinct, experience, and respect. It came from watching, listening, and learning through the generations. Now so many have drifted away from that connection, viewing plants as nothing more than a resource to be used, or a backdrop to human life. And in doing so, we have lost a part of ourselves.

Reconnecting with the Green is not just about learning, it is about remembering. It is about stepping back into a relationship that was never truly broken, only forgotten. It is about seeing plants not as passive things but as living, breathing beings that nourish, heal, and sustain us. When we rekindle this bond, we do not just grow in knowledge, we grow in spirit. We rediscover our place in the world, not as rulers over nature, but as a part of it, as we were always meant to be.

A major change in our relationship occurred in the early part of the twentieth century, when humans gave up control of their food; that is by handing it over to multinationals. The change had come about primarily because of the invention of factory culture. People were taken into the factories to provide labour for the newly emerging capitalist society, and this resulted in people having less time to tend gardens and farmland. Therefore the production of food became industrialised in response to greater needs.

Big corporations took over food production, churning it out on a massive scale. In the process, traditional, nature-based ways of growing and preparing food started to fade away. What was once a deeply connected mindful practice became another industry, stripping away the relationship between people, plants, and the land.

Another vital loss was our deep connection to planetary cycles and the seasons, both essential to food production. As industrialisation took over, a massive disconnect formed between the human psyche and the natural world. We drifted away from Nature, lulled into complacency by corporations that convinced us they could think for us. This illusion has led many to believe that we *control* nature rather than recognise the truth: we are not its masters but its co-workers and beneficiaries. The real wisdom lies in understanding our place within the greater web of life, not above it.

There is a darker, more malefic edge to severing this bond, when control over food becomes control over people. When an individual's access to nourishment is dictated by distant hands, their will is softened, their choices narrowed, their dependence deepened. Hunger is a powerful force; when faced with starvation, dignity is easily traded for survival. History bears witness to this cruel truth.

Take the Irish Famine, an entire people stripped of sustenance, left to the mercy of soup kitchens and workhouses, forced to abandon their homeland in search of survival. Many who crossed the ocean in desperation found themselves caught in another trap, not saved but exploited, reduced to little more than a cheap, disposable labour force for the New World. This is the shadow side of disconnection when the Green is taken from us: so too is our freedom.

Today control takes a different form. We are not starving—we are drowning in excess. Supermarkets overflow with abundance: fruits, vegetables, and meats from every corner of the world line the shelves year-round. Yet beneath this illusion of plenty lies a fragile, unsustainable system. In the UK, our food production is failing to support us, and so we have become utterly reliant on being employees to afford it, on imports to sustain it, and on a network that stretches far beyond our reach.

More troubling still, we have lost sight of what we are actually eating. The connection to our food—where it comes from, how it is grown, the lives of the plants and animals that nourish us—has been severed. We no longer ask the questions we once did, no longer demand to know the truth of our own sustenance. And in this silence our plates have been filled with chemicals, with medicines, with unseen interventions that shape our bodies and minds in ways we barely comprehend. What was once nourishment has become something else entirely.

And yet, for all this excess, what do we truly need? Not forty-five different tins of beans, not an endless parade of brands vying for attention. In reality, we only need choice between two versions of the same thing—one simple decision, not an illusion of abundance designed to distract us from the deeper issues at play. We don't need a hundred varieties of packaging, we just need beans. Real food. Honest food. The kind that nourishes rather than exploits.

There's a thought experiment that lays bare just how much control over our own survival we've surrendered. Imagine this, a disaster strikes. There are no cars, no electricity to preserve or cook food, no access to a grocery shop. Where is your next meal coming from? Look around—can you find a steady, reliable, and nutritious source of food?

Now, take it further. What about winter? Can you still feed yourself when the trees are bare, the fields frozen, the days short and unforgiving?

And what about water? Not your tap, that's dry. Not your toilet, that's unsafe. Where is your nearest clean water source? Can you get to it, carry enough, and ensure it's drinkable?

Now for the bad news: odds are, you have no answer to these questions. You likely live in a town or city, a death trap in any true crisis. You probably don't know which plants around you are edible or how to find, kill, and butcher an animal. And that's the stark reality: without food and water, you are already lost.

This is the power you have handed over, to Tesco, to Sainsbury's, to the government, to commodity providers, to landlords, and, ultimately, to those who hold the keys to your survival. You can only live three days without water. And that old adage, that we are all just three meals away from chaos, from desperation, from violence, isn't just a grim saying. It's the truth.

Cheery stuff, indeed.

CHAPTER TWO

The biology of the green

To exploit something for profit, we must first strip it of its identity, worth, and very life. And that's precisely what we've done. I use the term *human* here to describe all living beings. History has shown us that the worst atrocities—slavery, genocide, and oppression—come from dehumanising others, turning them into objects instead of sentient beings. Plants are some of the oldest victims of this.

Look at how we treat forests; not as rich, living ecosystems but as wasted space unless cleared for farmland. Weeds? Just plants in the wrong place, killed without a second thought. Herbs? A threat to pharmaceutical companies because they offer natural remedies that can't be patented and sold. In this mindset, plants only exist to serve human demands, and if they don't fit into that framework, they're wiped out without hesitation.

Nowhere is this more evident than in the destructive practice of monoculture farming, the industrial approach of growing a single crop over vast areas of land. This method is a direct assault on biodiversity, stripping landscapes of the rich, interwoven relationships between different species that keep ecosystems balanced. When you plant only one crop, you create an ecological dead zone: pollinators lose their habitats, predator species disappear, and pests thrive without natural checks.

Farmers then drench their fields in pesticides, killing unwanted insects yet the very ones essential for a healthy ecosystem.

But that's just the beginning. Monoculture destroys the soil itself. In a healthy environment, diverse plant life pulls different nutrients from the earth while others return them, keeping the land fertile. But when only one species grows, it continually strips the same minerals, exhausting the soil until it becomes barren. To keep crops alive, farmers flood the land with synthetic fertilisers, temporary fixes that further disrupt the delicate web of underground life. Without deep-rooted plants to hold the ground together, soil erosion accelerates, washing away what little fertility remains. And when the land can no longer produce, more forests are cut down, more wild spaces bulldozed, and the cycle repeats.

The damage doesn't stop at the soil. Monoculture is also a major driver of water scarcity and pollution. These large-scale farms demand an enormous amount of irrigation, draining rivers, lakes, and underground aquifers far faster than they can replenish. And all those fertilisers, pesticides, and herbicides? They don't just stay in the fields, they seep into water systems, poisoning everything downstream. This runoff causes massive algal blooms in lakes and oceans, suffocating marine life by depleting oxygen levels, killing fish, and throwing entire aquatic ecosystems into chaos.

And then there's the climate vulnerability monoculture creates. Nature thrives on diversity because it allows ecosystems to adapt. A mix of plants means that if one species struggles due to drought, pests, or disease, others take its place and keep the system stable. But monoculture offers no such resilience. When every plant is genetically identical, a disease outbreak can wipe out an entire crop, leading to devastating food shortages.

This isn't just about farmland, it's about destroying entire ecosystems. Rainforests, wetlands, and grasslands are being razed at an alarming rate to make room for monoculture crops, particularly soy (used for cattle feed), palm oil, and biofuels. What was once thriving biodiverse land is now endless lifeless rows of a single species. We bulldoze rainforests to make way for cattle pastures, only to slaughter the animals en masse. And in a dark twist of irony, we're now destroying forests in a frenzied hunt for rare minerals—fuelling the so-called "eco-friendly" revolution. These resources power our phones, devices, and, most alarmingly, our electric cars, marketed as green alternatives. At the same time, the devastation behind them remains hidden from view by greenwashing and other gaslighting techniques.

Monoculture isn't just a farming method; it's a mindset, a reflection of our disconnection from the natural world. It's the idea that plants, soil, water, and life itself are commodities to be controlled and exploited rather than sacred parts of a greater whole. If we truly want to live in balance with nature, we must move beyond this destructive system. We must return to regenerative, biodiverse farming, where the land is nurtured rather than depleted, and where food production works *with* nature instead of against it.

The real path forward isn't about domination, it's about partnership. It's about remembering that we are not separate from nature but deeply intertwined with it. And if we fail to recognise that, the consequences will be far more devastating than just the loss of a few forests or a handful of species. It will be the loss of the very systems that sustain life itself.

What causes plant blindness

One of the main reasons we become "plant blind", disregarding plants as sentient beings, is because they appear rooted in one place, seemingly unable to move as animals do. Yet, once we begin to engage more thoughtfully with scientific research, we uncover an entirely different story, one that challenges our assumptions about plant intelligence and awareness. As ecologist Richard Karban of the University of California laments, "I think most people regard plants as being pretty unresponsive and stuck in one place ... Now, animals, they're interesting because they can change and act in response to their environment." This bias blinds us to the fact that plants are not passive; instead, they are deeply responsive to their surroundings in ways that we are only beginning to understand.

We struggle with the field of reference because we cannot help but anthropomorphise, measuring them against ourselves. In doing so, we see them as weak organisms, lacking a brain, a heart, or any means of locomotion. As a result, we superimpose our limitations onto them, imagining what it would be like to exist without these traits rather than recognising that plants have evolved along an entirely different path.

Unlike animals, plants have evolved to thrive in one place, developing a modular structure that helps them survive predators and environmental pressures in ways that challenge our usual ideas about survival. It's a remarkable feat of evolution. As Stefano Mancuso explains, plants have a "Lego-like" biology—cut them apart, and from each severed piece, a new plant can grow.[2] This strategy means that even when parts of a plant are eaten or damaged, it can keep going. Instead of relying on a single, centralised system to control everything, plants spread their intelligence and vitality throughout their entire being, making them far more resilient than we often realise.

And it's exactly this resilience that leads to misunderstanding. We tend to assume intelligence needs a brain, a central control hub, because that's how it works for us. If a human or animal loses a vital organ, survival isn't an option, but a plant can lose huge parts of itself and still flourish. That doesn't mean plants lack intelligence or awareness; it just means they operate differently. We need to move beyond the idea that our way of experiencing the world is the only way and start recognising the sheer brilliance of plant life on its own terms.

Plants have all the senses we do, just not housed in the kind of structures we'd recognise. Their "brain" isn't in a "head", they don't have a face, their "stomachs" aren't in an abdomen, and their reproductive organs aren't between their legs. Yet they still breathe without lungs, "eat" and nourish themselves without a digestive system, and make decisions without a physical brain.

Because their way of being is so radically different from ours, we tend to ignore it rather than try to understand and appreciate it. This has left us "plant blind". But if we want to truly connect with and deepen our relationship with our plant kin, we need to find a point of reference that helps us recognise our shared existence and strengthens our symbiosis with the plants, our fellow beings.

Circulation and communication combine

Plants have a circulatory system that runs from the plant's root to the leaf's tip. This system is the equivalent to our own circulation of blood and the transportation of food and water. *Xylem*, the interior tissue of the plant system, transports water and minerals up the plant, from root to leaf, whilst *Phloem* transports the sugars made by photosynthesis down from the leaf to the root. The Xylem is also a conductive tissue that allows the passage of electrical impulses throughout the plant.

---

[2] Mancuso and Viola, *Brilliant green: the surprising history and science of plant intelligence*; Mancuso and Viola, *Brilliant green: the surprising history and science of plant intelligence*.

Plants do not have specialised cells like neurons, but they maintain an electrical signalling mechanism that allows the rapid dissemination of signals up and down the plant. Plants also have a mechanism like our endocrine system, which slowly diffuses chemicals that travel between cells but can also pass messages to neighbours. You might also be surprised to learn that plants have all our "senses", and some extra ones on top.

Plant sight

It is true that plants don't have eyes, but they do have some of the most photosensitive reactions on the planet. Green plants spend their day seeking light, their primary food source, and they move towards it with the determination of a cannabis smoker seeking cheese puffs.

That we don't see the movement of the plant is a problem because the movement is itself outside our temporal understanding. What I mean by this is that plants experience and thereby react to linear time in a totally different way from us. So, let's compare the concept of our linear day (24 hour clock) to that of a typical "day in the life" of a tree:

A. *Our typical day*

Morning: Wake up, get up, wash, put on clothes (I hope!), and we go to work ...

Afternoon: Have lunch, back to work ...

Evening: Go home, have tea and relax ...

Nighttime: Take off clothes, go to bed ... and sleep!

All this activity takes 24 hours.

B. *Plant's typical "day"*

For trees and green plants, it is a much slower process: *Morning:* (spring) Wake up, start to put on clothes, bud and develop leaves and do work (photosynthesis)

Afternoon: (summer) Most productive, working away and eating as we go ...

Evening: (autumn) Now full of food, slowing down, getting sleepy, and starting to change clothes (withdrawal of chlorophyll and leaf loss).

Night: (winter) All clothes changed, everything is drawn in, and sleep begins.

So, I hear you say, what's the difference? Now, I want you to imagine your reaction when a fly buzzes around your head. If it's not bothering you, do you notice it? No, you don't; that is because its time-space is much faster than yours, and in the same way, ours is much quicker than that of the tree. For this reason, it takes much longer to form a relationship with a tree compared to a plant. Herbs and flowers have a daily cycle as well as an annual one. In my experience of magically working with trees, they tend to have an annual period only, but are responsive and useful as our allies in other ways.

Our ability to see this time difference in plant movement has been challenged recently. You can find amazing time-lapse videos of plants practically dancing. Plants use phototropism—literally, movement towards light—by detecting even the tiniest amounts of light with specialised receptors. These receptors allow them to shift and align themselves towards the best food source. But here's the fascinating part: these light receptors aren't confined to one place, they exist in every single cell. So, plants don't have eyes, they *are* eyes!

Communication and community

Plants communicate via chemicals called *Volatile Organic Compounds*, VOC for short. These chemicals are transmitted through the air and from their root tips, and facilitate communication similarly to animals' endocrine or hormonal system.

In Dan Cossins' article *Plant Talk*, he examines the details of an experiment performed in 2009:

> It's every plant's worst nightmare ... In the fall of 2009, in a Victorian greenhouse at the Cruickshank Botanic Garden at the University of Aberdeen in Scotland, Zdenka Babikova sprinkled vegetation-devouring aphids on eight broad bean plants and sealed each plant's leaves and stems inside a clear plastic bag. This was no act of malice, though; it was all in the name of science.

Babikova, a PhD student at the University of Aberdeen, knew that aphid infested bean plants release odorous chemicals known as volatile organic compounds (VOCs) into the air to warn their neighbours, which respond by emitting different VOCs that repel aphids and attract aphid-hunting wasps. What she didn't know was whether the plants were also sounding the alarm beneath the soil surface … Five weeks earlier, Babikova filled eight thirty centimetre diameter pots with soil containing Glomus intraradices, a mycorrhizal fungus that connects the roots of plants with its hyphae, the branching filaments that make up the fungal mycelium. Like a subterranean swap meet, these hyphal networks facilitate the trade of nutrients between fungi and plants. In each pot, Babikova planted five broad bean plants: a "donor" plant surrounded by four "receiver" plants. One of the receivers was allowed to form root and mycorrhizal contact with the donor; another formed mycorrhizal contact only, and two more had neither root nor mycorrhizal contact. Once the mycorrhizal networks were well established, Babikova infested the donor plants with aphids and sealed each plant in a separate plastic bag that allowed for the passage of carbon dioxide, water, and water vapor but blocked larger molecules, such as the VOCs used for airborne communication … Four days later, Babikova placed individual aphids or parasitoid wasps in spherical choice chambers to see how they reacted to the VOC bouquets collected from receiver plants. Sure enough, only plants that had mycorrhizal connections to the infested plant were repellent to aphids and attractive to wasps, an indication that the plants were in fact using their fungal symbionts to send warnings.[3]

Plenty of scientific studies have shown that plant communication, both within their own species and across different species, is incredibly complex and actively influences their behaviour. But why is this seen as so different from me warning a friend not to walk down a certain path because a wasps' nest is on the road? Communication changes behaviour; my friend listens, avoids the nest, and does not get stung. In the same way, plant communication shifts their behaviour, helping them avoid damage or being eaten.

---

[3] Dan Cossins, "Plant Talk," *The Scientist* 28, no. 1 (2014), https://www.the-scientist.com/plant-talk-38209.

So why am I considered conscious and intelligent for recognising danger and warning someone, yet a plant doing something similar is not given the same recognition?

Plants communicate with animals all the time. Take, for example, a herbivorous mite attacking a plant; the plant picks up on the damage and sends signals to the rest of its body. Then, it releases pheromones that attract predatory mites, the very creatures that will hunt and eat the herbivorous mites. Essentially the plant is working with the idea that "the enemy of my enemy is my friend". But to do this, it must *know* the difference between friend and foe; it must recognise itself as separate from others. That means plants are not just passively reacting; they are making conscious decisions to act.

And that brings us to sentience. Sentience is simply the ability to perceive or experience subjectively. In other words, it is about recognising that others exist as something separate from oneself. "I am, because I am not them". If that is the case, then perhaps it is time we start acknowledging that plants are far more aware than we give them credit for.

The semantics of intelligence and sentience

Scientists have a relatively minimal definition of intelligence. *The Oxford English Dictionary* defines it as "the ability to learn, understand and think logically about things". Oddly enough, humans have no trouble discussing intelligence, even when it comes to artificial intelligence. Yet they struggle to accept the possibility that plants might also be intelligent and, by extension, sentient.

Dr Monica Gagliano, in her book *Thus Spoke the Plant*, provides fascinating evidence for this idea. She conducted experiments with the Mimosa plant, which responded in unexpected ways when subjected to what is known as "the Drop Test".[4]

The Drop Test is typically used to assess animals' awareness of proprioception and danger. It works by measuring their reflex actions versus non-reactive behaviour, whether they recognise that they are no longer at risk. Scientists have long understood that when an action is repeated enough, an animal's response shifts from being controlled by the *autonomic nervous system*, which operates involuntarily to prevent

---

[4] PhD Monica Gagliano, *Thus Spoke the Plant*. (United States of America: North Atlantic Books, 2018).

harm, to the *voluntary nervous system*, which involves conscious decision-making. This transition is key because it prevents unnecessary energy loss through involuntary movements.

Rats are commonly used as scientific models for behavioural studies, including those related to humans. It is well recognised that rats possess high intelligence and communicative sentience. Typically, a rat subjected to the Drop Test will take about seven drops before its reflex action normalises into a non-reactive state. However, rats do not retain a memory of this response, so when tested again the next day, they react as if experiencing the drop for the first time.

Dr Gagliano carried out similar experiments using the Mimosa plant, which folds its leaves when exposed to danger, a mechanism that prevents damage and reduces water loss. She tested two groups of plants, one deprived of light, unable to photosynthesise, and another allowed to photosynthesise freely. The folding reflex is costly in terms of energy and interferes with the plant's ability to absorb light.

Incredibly, she found that both groups of plants stopped closing their leaves after about five drops, suggesting that they had *learned* there was no real danger. Even more astonishing was that the light-deprived plants learned this information more quickly than those able to photosynthesise as they prioritised energy conservation more effectively.

A week later, she repeated the experiment. The plants did not react. This strongly suggests that they had a *memory* of the previous experience and could retrieve and apply that information.

Despite the groundbreaking nature of this research, it has gone largely unreported, perhaps because humans resist attributing intelligence or sentience to plants, preferring instead to reserve such traits for our own species. Yet recognising sentience in plants forces us to rethink our own perceived dominance in the hierarchy of life.

Communicating with plants

There is ample evidence, particularly from interviews with indigenous peoples, that highlights the significance of plant communication. For centuries shamans have engaged in direct dialogue with plants, reinforcing plants' central role in their spiritual and ecological understanding.

One particularly compelling study, *The Concept of Plants as Teachers among Four Mestizo Shamans of Iquitos, North-Eastern Peru* by Luis Eduardo Luna, documents how shamans describe the source of their knowledge. When asked where their wisdom originates, they all responded in the same way, "the purgative itself teaches you", referring to the ayahuasca brew.[5]

There are countless scientific studies on the ingestion of entheogens, substances that facilitate an experience of "the divine within". Kenneth Tupper, for example, explores the connection between shamans and ayahuasca, whose name translates to "Vine of the Soul", a direct reference to its spiritual significance.[6]

One of the most transformative works I have ever read is by Stephen Harrod Buhner. His way of describing the personality of plants and how they communicate was a deeply personal experience for me; it reflected so much of my relationship with the plants I work with. Yet, even as I read, I could hear those doubt demons whispering in my ear. I remember sitting in my garden, book in hand, listening to Buhner speak about his experiences, and those of the indigenous peoples he had worked with.

And then something remarkable happened. His words unlocked something deep within me; I found myself sobbing, overwhelmed with joy. It was the sheer relief of knowing that I was not alone, that others too had walked this path, experienced this magic, and rediscovered a connection so many have forgotten.

The wild mind: The psychology of Green places

There have been numerous studies on the effect of being in the wild. Science calls it forest bathing—*Shinrin-yoku* in Japanese—the act of immersing oneself in the Green, of simply being among the leaves, allowing the mind to soften, the body to settle. It is not exercise, not a task to be completed, but a return, a remembering. Studies tell us that time spent in wild places lowers cortisol, steadies the heart, and soothes the nervous system like a lullaby hummed by the land itself. But we don't need studies to know the truth of it. We have felt it, even if only in passing, in the way grief eases beneath towering oaks, the way stress loses its edges when wrapped in the scent of pine and damp earth.

---

[5] Luis Eduardo Luna, "The concept of plants as teachers among four mestizo shamans of Iquitos, northeastern Peru," *Journal of ethnopharmacology* 11, no. 2 (1984).

[6] Kenneth W. Tupper, "Entheogens and Existential Intelligence: The Use of Plant Teachers as Cognitive Tools," *Canadian Journal of Education/Revue canadienne de l'éducation* 27, no. 4 (2002), https://doi.org/10.2307/1602247, http://www.jstor.org/stable/1602247.

Step beneath the canopy, let the hush settle over you. The air is different here; thicker, richer, humming with a life older than human memory. Dappled light dances on the forest floor, shifting and swaying like breath, like tide. And something in you shifts with it.

Trees alter us. Not just through air and breath, but through something deeper, something woven into our bones. Their stillness slows our racing thoughts; their quiet presence reminds us how to listen, how to be. Here, among the roots and the wind-stirred branches, the mind loosens its grip on worry, and the weight of the modern world dissolves into birdsong and leaf-rustle. Joy is easier here. It creeps in gently, without fanfare. The light filtering through birch leaves, the glimmer of a beetle's shell, the sudden burst of foxgloves on a mossy bank. The wild does not ask anything of us. It does not demand productivity, does not measure worth. It simply is. And in its presence, we too are allowed to simply be.

So step into the Green, and let it do what it has always done: mend, nourish, and remind you that you were never meant to live apart from it.

Trees, plants, and the Divine

To understand how we came to this fractured place, it is worth turning our gaze to the Divine, to the stories, myths, and beliefs that have shaped how we see the world. Particularly within Christianity, perspectives on God and dominion have cast long shadows over our relationship with the land, rippling outward through centuries of thought and action. At the root of it all, there is a question rarely asked—how has our understanding of the sacred shaped the crisis we now face?

In the great mythologies of the Abrahamic faiths, Judaism, Christianity, and Islam, two trees stand at the heart of humanity's awakening, and, depending on interpretation, its fall. The Tree of Knowledge of Good and Evil and the Tree of Life are not merely props in the story of Genesis; they are profound symbols of transformation, consciousness, and the sacred relationship between humans and the wild world. Yet, despite their deep esoteric significance, they are often reduced to a moral tale, a cautionary whisper about transgression and obedience.

Christian doctrine has long fixated on Eve's perceived sin, her grasping for knowledge and her defiance, while other figures like Lilith slip conveniently from the narrative. The broader role of trees and plants in sacred tradition is largely overlooked, their wisdom buried beneath centuries of rigid doctrine. But step outside the confines of this narrow retelling, and you find a different story—one where trees are not simply witnesses to divine encounters but active participants in enlightenment.

In the *Bhagavad Gita*, there is Ashvattha, the sacred fig tree, whose roots stretch beyond time itself, embodying both the eternal and the mortal self. The Buddha's awakening came beneath the Bodhi Tree, its leaves rustling with the secrets of liberation. In the Norse tradition, Yggdrasil, the great World Tree, stands at the centre of existence, and it was upon its branches that Odin hung for three days and nights to claim the runes, knowledge bought with suffering, wisdom drawn from the marrow of the tree itself.

And then there is the Kabbalistic Tree of Life, its thirty-two paths mapping the ascent of the soul, a structure so profound that it later wove its way into western esoteric traditions, influencing the Tarot and shaping the mystical pursuit of hidden truths.

These trees are not passive. They do not merely decorate the edges of sacred texts, they are the revelation. They stand at the crossroads of matter and spirit, of body and wisdom, of what is seen and what is beyond sight. And yet, in much of modern thought, they have been stripped of their voice, reduced to symbols rather than sacred presences.

But trees do not forget. Their roots stretch through time, and their branches cradle the sky. Their wisdom is written in leaves, in sap, in the patient unfurling of life itself. Perhaps, as we seek to reclaim our connection to the Green, it is time to listen once more. Perhaps the trees have been waiting for us to remember.

Yet somewhere along the way we forgot. We severed the sacred from the soil, lifted the Divine into the heavens and left the earth behind. We placed spirit above matter, humanity above nature, progress above balance. And in doing so, we lost something vital.

The disconnect between western religion and indigenous wisdom

The absence of trees and plants in mainstream religious thought is more than an oversight, it is a symptom of a deeper fracture, a profound disconnect between the dominant western worldview and the wisdom held by indigenous traditions. Meanwhile many indigenous cultures have never forgotten the intelligence of the plant world, continuing to listen, to honour, to work in deep reciprocity with the Green.

Western thought has too often dismissed such knowledge as primitive, unscientific, and irrelevant.

But let's be clear: this dismissal is not simply about science or progress. It is rooted in something older, something far more insidious. I believe this disregard is born from an ingrained and often unexamined racial bias. The assumption lingers that if a culture does not conform to the structures of industrialisation, if it does not measure success in terms of commercial gain, then its knowledge, no matter how effective, no matter how deeply attuned to the living world, is deemed lesser, unworthy of serious consideration.

This is the shadow of colonialism, the legacy of the Industrial Revolution, both of which carried the same doctrine: that so-called civilised societies had the right, perhaps even the duty, to dominate nature rather than live in harmony with it. The land was seen as a resource, a thing to be owned, divided, and extracted from. The sacred relationship between humans and the wild was severed, and in its place a culture of control took root, one that persists, despite all claims of enlightenment, despite all our so-called progress.

Even now, in an era of sustainability pledges and greenwashed promises, the old patterns remain. Tech giants, corporations, and governments speak of reforestation, of carbon offsets, of eco-conscious initiatives, but the question remains—do they truly care for balance, reciprocity, and the sacred dance of life? Or is this just another mask, another illusion, designed to maintain the same relentless cycle of exploitation and control?

Look closely at our relationship with the Green, and an old wound emerges, a deep, insidious pattern that has shaped how we think, not just about plants and animals, but about each other. At its root lies hierarchy, the belief that some stand above while others must kneel below. It is a way of thinking so old and entrenched that it often goes unnoticed, woven as it is into philosophy, religion, and the very bones of our civilisation.

The idea of a cosmic order, where everything has its place, is ancient. The early Greek thinkers, even before Plato and Aristotle, imagined a world where humanity sat at the pinnacle of nature, just beneath the gods, with animals and plants trailing somewhere far below. This Great Chain of Being shaped the philosophies that followed, embedding the idea that domination was not only necessary but natural.

With the rise of Christianity and Islam, this belief took on divine weight. Genesis 1:28 gave Adam dominion over all life, reinforcing the idea that the earth existed solely for human use. Lynn White Jr., in *The Historical Roots of Our Ecological Crisis*, argues that Christianity, more than any other religion, severed humanity from the natural world. In this worldview, God was no longer in nature but above it, an absentee creator, a distant judge. Nature, stripped of its sacredness, was something to be ruled, tamed, and controlled.[7]

And what of those who lived differently? Those who saw the land as kin, who worked with the intelligence of plants rather than against it? Their knowledge was dismissed, their traditions labelled primitive, and their voices silenced beneath the weight of Western expansion. Colonialism, industrialism, and religious dogma worked hand in hand to erase indigenous wisdom, enforcing the belief that a culture's worth was measured by its ability to consume, conquer, and commercialise.

This pattern of domination extended far beyond the land. The same dualistic thinking that placed humans over nature also placed men over women, logic over intuition, spirit over matter. Val Plumwood calls this the "hyper-separation" of mind from body, and reason from feeling. The western world built itself on these oppositions, shaping institutions that dismissed the living world as passive, as something to be owned, controlled, and reshaped at will.[8]

Yet, even in the so-called Age of Enlightenment, where science claimed to replace superstition, the pattern remained. The rise of rational theology and mechanistic science in the eighteenth century marked another turning point. Nature was no longer seen as an entity with its own will but as a vast machine, a lifeless mechanism operating under fixed laws. Newton's universe functioned like clockwork, and with this vision came the idea of mastery, of bending the earth to our will, of breaking it apart and reassembling it as we pleased.

William Blake saw it happening in his own time. He watched as England's "Green and Pleasant Land" was swallowed by "Dark Satanic Mills", the relentless machinery of progress grinding away at something ancient and sacred. The Romantics knew, even then, that something

---

[7] Lynn White, "The Historical Roots of Our Ecologic Crisis," *Science* 155, no. 3767 (1967), http://www.jstor.org/stable/1720120.
[8] Val Plumwood, "Gender,Eco-Feminism and The Environment," in *Controversies in Environmental Sociology.*, ed. Rob White (United States of America: Cambridge University Press, 2004).

had been lost, that the deep reciprocal bond between humans and the living world had been severed. But by then the machine was in motion, and we have not stopped it since.

And so here we are, standing at the precipice of ecological collapse, the consequences of this ancient arrogance finally catching up with us. We have burned, extracted, and poisoned, believing ourselves above consequence and the laws of nature. But the trees remember. The land remembers. The question is do we?

If we are to find our way back, we must begin by dismantling the illusions that have led us here. The idea that we are separate. The belief that we stand above. The lie that the Green is ours to use, rather than ours to belong to. The trees were never beneath us. The earth was never ours to own. It is time to listen, to relearn, to return, before it is too late.

Animism—A light within

Even as the mechanistic worldview tightened its grip, and nature was stripped of its soul and reduced to lifeless matter, the older ways of knowing never truly disappeared. Animism, the whisper of the wild and heartbeat of the land, endured. It is one of the oldest ways of seeing, a thread that runs deep through human history, binding us to the earth, to the trees, and to the rivers that still murmur with memory.

Unlike the rigid logic of mechanistic thought, which insists that only the human mind possesses awareness, Animism recognises the deep sentience of all things. The land is not dead, silent, or inert. The trees are not timber waiting to be felled, nor the rivers mere resources to be drained. They are voices, presences, forces woven into the same vast web of being that we are. Where the modern world sees landscapes as things to be owned and controlled, Animism understands them as kin: alive, aware, and deeply entangled with us in ways we have forgotten.

For those who see through animist eyes, nature is not a machine, ticking along in predictable patterns. The world breathes. The forests speak in rustling leaves, the stones hum with the weight of time, and the wind carries the laughter of spirits who have never left. This understanding is not new, it is ancient. As anthropologist Leslie E. Sponsel points out, the belief in inspirited nature dates back 60,000 to 80,000 years, perhaps even to our Neanderthal ancestors. This is not a quaint relic of the past; it is the foundation upon which human spirituality was built.

The term Animism was first coined by Edward Tylor in *Primitive Culture*, where he described it as the root of all early religious thought, the common thread linking indigenous traditions to the world's great faiths. He called it a doctrine of universal vitality, the recognition that life is not confined to flesh, and that spirit is not something separate from matter, but something woven through it.

Science, in its unrelenting quest for understanding, has long relied on the technique of breaking things apart—dissecting bodies, isolating molecules, splitting atoms. The belief is simple: if we can unravel the pieces, we can understand the whole. And yet I would argue that this approach is, at best, only partially true.

A bird, when taken apart, reveals its organs, its chemistry, the intricate mechanics of its wings. But no scalpel, microscope, or algorithm can tell us why it sings. No dissection can explain the quiet joy that drives it to feed its young, or the deep, instinctive pull that sends it soaring across vast distances, trusting the rhythms of wind and season. The animating force, the essence of life itself, remains elusive, unmeasurable, unquantifiable, and, perhaps most troubling to the scientific mind, unacknowledged.

Modern education continues to teach that the universe is a vast, mechanical system, a place of cause and effect, and clockwork precision. Stephen Buhner, in his work on plant-human relationships, speaks of the loss of Biophilia, our deep, instinctive love for the wild. He argues that this disconnection is not just an accident, it is engineered. Children today know more species through television screens than through their own eyes; they can name exotic animals from books but have never felt the damp breath of a forest morning, never sat in the hush of old trees and listened.

And so they grow up as outsiders to nature, separate from the land that feeds them. They are taught to see the world as a collection of objects rather than a living, breathing web of interconnection. Is it any wonder then that they do not care for what they have never known? How can we expect them to protect the Green when they have never truly met it?

If we are to heal this wound, we must do more than teach sustainability; we must rekindle reverence. Those who have not yet joined us in Unveiling the Green must come to understand what our ancestors knew so well: that to love the land is to remember ourselves. That without this relationship, we will not survive.

Robin Wall Kimmerer, in her work on indigenous knowledge, offers a different perspective, one that recognises indigenous traditions not as relics of the past, but as essential roadmaps to the future. She writes, "Traditional knowledge can give us insight into the practice and belief concerning the relationship of living beings to one another and the physical environment".

This is not a small thing. It is not a footnote in history. It is a blueprint for survival.

Among the Ojibwe people, for example, all living beings are seen as Persons, not just humans, but bears, trees, stones, rivers. Everything holds agency, awareness, and intrinsic worth. This perspective, so different from the Western tendency to classify nature as a resource, offers a model for true sustainability. Not as an economic strategy, not as a corporate buzzword, but as a way of living in right relationship with the world. This understanding has always been there, waiting. The question is, will we listen?

The war on intuitive medicine

For as long as humans have walked the earth, plants have been our healers. Herbal medicine is not an alternative practice—it is the foundation upon which all medicine was built. From the temples of Ancient Egypt to the apothecaries of medieval Europe, from indigenous shamans to village herbalists, the wisdom of the Green has been passed down, whispered from leaf to hand to lips.

Yet, in the age of pharmaceuticals, this knowledge has been cast aside, dismissed as folklore while the very same plants are stripped down to their chemical components, repackaged, and sold back to us as modern medicine. The bias is not accidental, it is part of a wider pattern, the systematic erasure of traditional knowledge, the industrialisation of healing, and the transformation of medicine from a relationship into a product.

A century ago, the most powerful drugs were all plant-based. Aspirin from meadowsweet. Digoxin from foxglove. Quinine from cinchona bark. Morphine from the opium poppy. Even today pharmaceutical companies comb the rainforests, harvesting knowledge from indigenous healers, yet those healers are rarely credited, let alone compensated.

Ethnobotanist Nina Etkin describes the common attitude of western researchers, who often regard indigenous herbalists as "secretive, uncooperative, or simply wrong"[9] There is a deep irony in this. The same corporations that dismiss traditional medicine as unscientific are the first to patent its discoveries. They do not disbelieve in the power of plants—they simply wish to own it.

But there is a fundamental difference between the pharmaceutical approach and the way of the Green. Pharmaceutical medicine treats symptoms; herbal medicine seeks to heal the root cause of the disease. Modern science isolates active compounds, extracting what it deems useful while discarding the rest. Herbalists, by contrast, use the whole plant, understanding that nature does not work in fragments, but in harmony.

Take the dandelion. Pharmaceutical science studies its chemical components, isolating those that affect bile production, creating synthetic versions to treat gallstones. But an intuitive herbalist sees something deeper. Nathaniel Hughes describes Dandelion as a teacher, a plant for those who struggle to assert themselves, for those whose kindness has turned to self-erasure.

To work with Dandelion is to heal not just the body, but the spirit. This is what modern medicine has forgotten: plants do not simply fix us. They teach us.

The living intelligence of the green

We have been taught that plants are passive, that they exist without thought, without will. This is a lie.

Plants listen. They respond. They learn. They communicate in ways that science is only beginning to grasp. Mycorrhizal networks, what some call the Wood Wide Web, allow trees to share nutrients and warnings. Plants shift their chemistry in response to threats, signalling distress in ways that others can understand. They do not perceive the world as we do, but they are aware. This is what the old traditions knew, what indigenous and more traditional cultures have never forgotten. That plants are not things. They are people.

The difference between the industrial worldview and the animist perspective is not simply one of belief, it is one of relationship.

---

[9] Nina L. Etkin, "Ethnopharmocology: Biobehavioral Approaches in the Anthropological Study of Indigenous Medicines," *Annual Review of Anthropology* 17 (1988), http://www.jstor.org/stable/2155904.

The pharmaceutical scientist sees a mushroom as a chemical factory, something to be extracted and refined. The shaman sees it as a teacher, a guide, a being to be approached with honour. This is not romanticism, or superstition. It is a different way of knowing.

If we are to reclaim our place within the Green, we must start here. We must dismantle the hierarchy that places humans at the top, above the trees, rivers, fungi, and stones. We must unlearn the arrogance that sees plants as mere objects, as lifeless matter to be studied, used, and discarded.

Because the truth is simple: the world is alive. It always has been. To hear it, we must listen. To understand it, we must remember. To heal, we must return.

This is the heart of Unveiling the Green, not just knowledge, but transformation. A way of seeing, a way of being, a way of belonging once more to the living world.

CHAPTER THREE

Tackling your world view

I am a scientist. I have an MSc in Applied Biology. I have spent years in research and development, working within the structures of academia, where evidence is king and where the world is neatly divided into measurable, quantifiable truths. I am also a pagan, an alchemist, and a witch. You might have noticed a bit of a clash in that list.

To say that these worlds have not always sat comfortably together would be an understatement. At times, they have forced me into impossible choices, leaving me questioning everything, even my own sanity. Science trained me to trust solid facts, to see through the lens of materialism and reductionism, to dismiss anything that could not be weighed, measured, or repeated under controlled conditions. Magic, on the other hand, demanded something different, a trust in experience, a knowing that is felt rather than proven, a willingness to engage with forces that slip beyond the confines of traditional logic. Reconciling these two perspectives has been one of the hardest battles of my life. At times I thought I had lost the plot completely. How do you hold scientific reason in one hand, and something as fluid, as intangible as magic in the other? How do you stand with your feet in two entirely different worlds, when neither wants to make room for the other?

And to make matters worse, there was the anthropocentrism, that deeply ingrained belief within science that humanity stands above all else, that intelligence belongs to us alone, and that the world exists as an object to be studied rather than a living, breathing force to be in relationship with. And honestly, I struggle to talk about it without absolutely losing my shit. It infuriates me because, as a species, we are utterly addicted to ourselves. We are so self-absorbed that we can barely see beyond our own reflection, so consumed with our own importance that we fail to recognise the vast web of intelligence surrounding us. If that isn't a full-blown narcissistic disorder, I don't know what is. And if we don't break free from this toxic self-obsession, and begin to listen to the world beyond ourselves, we are going to take everything down with us. This has to be rectified. And that starts with us, right now.

Stages of acceptance — is the work OK to do?

Before I could fully step into this work, I needed rules. Not to impose restrictions, but to give shape and structure to my own process, to create a framework that would allow me to navigate this path with clarity, integrity, and accountability. These principles became essential, not just for my own understanding, but to ensure that what I learned could be passed on to others.

These are my rules. They are not set in stone—take what resonates, adapt as needed—but abide by them.

Did it work for me?

Did the work provide concrete results, for my own or others' psychological and physical health?

✓ Yes? Then it is OK to do.

Did it bring satisfaction to the soul?

Did it result in well-being? Did it make me happier, more focused, more complete?

✓ Yes? Then it is OK to do.

Did the work prove to me that there are other "people" in the world?

And I do not mean "people" as we traditionally define them. I mean beings of intelligence, presence, and agency—ones who exist outside the human experience but who are very much real. Did these people communicate? Did they teach? Did they guide?

✓ Yes? Then it is OK to do.

And most importantly:

Do not waste time worrying about what others think.

If people think you are strange, eccentric, or even a witch—so be it. These labels have all been applied to me, and they will be applied to you too. If others do not understand why you do what you do, let them carry on with their lives. Let them stay in their comfortable narratives. You owe them no explanation.

Never try to justify your work.

Only a fool tries to explain an experience that exists beyond words. Your experience is yours. It does not need to match anyone else's. It does not need to be proven to anyone. It stands as it is, because it happened to you.

And yet, there will be others. Others who have walked this path before you. The more you engage with the Green World, the more you will notice something deeply unsettling, yet deeply beautiful, the growing awareness that you are not alone. The more you listen, the louder the voices become. The plants are speaking. The trees are speaking.

And what they are telling us is simple:

We are killing them.

If we do not start working together now, there will be no Green World left to speak with.

And if that happens, we are not just losing our medicines, our teachers, our kin. We are signing our own extinction notice.

Because here is the brutal truth: We are the most disposable of creatures.

Right now, we are entirely out of sync with the natural world. And while nature can and will survive without us, we cannot survive without it.

So, what do we do?

A method rooted in the old ways

The method we are using is an extended working derived from Charubel's original 1906 text, *The Psychology of Botany*,[10] later republished as the *Grimoire Sympathia* (The Workshop of the Infinite) in 2003.

While Charubel's grimoire laid the foundation, we have refined and expanded it, incorporating alchemy and astrological correspondences

---

[10] Charubel, *Psychology of Botany: A Treatise on Trees, Shrubs, and Plants, etc., for the Cure of Diseases and Ailments of the Human System, without Medicine, by Sympathy, Positive and Negative, on the Soul Plane* (Leigh: R. Welch, 1906). https://archive.org/details/PsychologyOfBotany.

to deepen the practice, creating an approach that is not just about plant magic but about true, reciprocal healing.

But before we delve into the practice itself, it is important to understand the man who first initiated this study.

Who was Charubel?

John Thomas, better known as Charubel, was a Welsh occultist born on November 6th 1826 in Montgomery. He came from a deeply Christian family, but his path led him far beyond the constraints of dogma. He was drawn to curative mesmerism and the esoteric arts, founding the Celestial Brotherhood, a lodge dedicated to astrology, herbalism, and mystical studies. Strangely, despite his Calvinist upbringing, Charubel was an animist, and he believed that every being, from the smallest stone to the tallest tree, had a soul and a spirit. To him true magic was accomplished not through domination, but through union, by joining one's spirit with the Divine. Though Charubel is best known for his astrological work, his beliefs on plant spirit medicine were radical for his time. In his own words:

> To become the subject of influence, we must first become sympathetically connected with that stone, plant, or tree—not by killing it, nor by reducing it to powders and pills, but by forming a bond, a fascination, a love. Whatever you greatly admire, whatever you love, you become receptive to. And what you love, you can be healed by.

This is no idle fantasy. This is not romanticism. This is knowledge as old as time itself. Though Charubel was bound by the colonial attitudes of his era, he held onto something rare and powerful, a belief in the Spirit Absolute in Nature. He knew what so many had forgotten: that healing is not about consumption. It is about relationship.

DragonOak and the Charubel method

I am the leader of the DragonOak Coven, a group based in South Wales, where for over thirty years, we have practised magic, performed rituals, and guided others along the winding paths of esoteric wisdom. For much of that time, we worked within the Western Mystery Tradition, structured, intellectual, and steeped in ritual precision.

Our work has always had depth. We have studied the Kabbalah, alchemy, planetary magic, and the Tarot; we have crafted tools, woven spells with cords, and worked the subtle forces of Hermetic practice. Many in DragonOak come from scientific backgrounds, so our approach naturally leaned toward the theoretical, the measured, and the disciplined.

And yet, something was missing. The real shift came when I began working with Mugwort. That was the moment of revelation, the sudden realisation that, for all our skill and knowledge, we were lacking something fundamental.

We were missing the Green.

Magic is more than structure; more than books, rituals, and symbols. It is alive; it pulses through the earth, through the chthonic depths, through the trees, the roots, and the fungi beneath our feet. For all our wisdom, we had barely scratched the surface of this living current.

Looking back, I can see how blind I was to the magic that lives in the land itself. The spirits, the forces, and the "People" who share this world with us had been overlooked. At the time, our coven's practice was formal and ceremonial: Middle Pillar rituals, precise circle castings, and astral work. Magic was something we performed with discipline and intellect, yet it was confined to the pages of books, rather than rooted in the soil beneath us. Now, everything has changed.

Gone are the days of structured, rigid rituals. No longer do we treat plant spirits as props, as symbolic tools to be used and discarded. Now, we work with them as allies, as teachers, as living presences with their own intelligence and will. We listen; we learn; we collaborate.

Our practice has deepened, becoming something raw and real. It is intuitive, emotional, interwoven with the land itself. This shift was not easy; some left, impatient for quicker results, unprepared for the slow, unfolding nature of Green Magic. They expected the instant power of ceremonial invocations and were unwilling to embrace the deep alchemy of transformation that working with the land requires. For those who stayed, who committed, who listened, and who allowed themselves to be changed, the rewards have been beyond words.

We are seekers, practitioners, and scholars. We are studying the Greek Magical Papyri, the old grimoires, and the wisdom of the ancients, refining our approach until intellect and spirit stand in harmony. I would put any of my Dragons against the best of the Western esoteric schools, not just in knowledge, but in depth and understanding.

We know our Geburah from our Gedulah; we have walked the paths of the Tree of Life and the Tree of Death. And yet, we do not seek our Gods in distant heavens. This is where we differ. We do not see the Divine as a distant figure sitting on a celestial throne, deciding the fate of mortals. The Divine is here, now; moving through the soil, through the roots, through the breath of the forest. It is in the fire that warms, in the river that carves the land, in the pulse of the Green that rises with the turning of the year. We do not stand beneath our Gods and Goddesses, begging for their attention. We stand beside them; as kin, as co-creators in the great work of existence. And when you feel that, when you experience it in your bones, when you move with the rhythms of the living world rather than standing apart from it, there is no going back. It is a knowing; deep and unshakable. It is a remembering.

I could not be prouder of my Dragons; those who have pushed beyond the barriers of tradition and rekindled their animistic connection to the Divine, right here, in the green fields that breathe and pulse with life.

So, if this speaks to you, if you feel the pull, if you sense something wilder and deeper calling to you, then come walk with us. This is a journey like no other.

The five pillars of working with plant spirits

When working with plants in a magical, alchemical, and spiritual context, we must approach them as living beings with their own intelligence, energy, and purpose. This is not a process of simple use or extraction; it is a relationship, a collaboration, and a deep immersion into the Green Mysteries. To truly understand a plant, we must work with it across multiple dimensions. Each aspect informs the next, weaving together into a holistic practice that is both practical and mystical.

The physical: growing with intention

This is where the relationship begins—with the soil, the seed, and the cycle of life. Whether working with a food crop or a medicinal herb, understanding the plant's physical needs is essential.

When to plant, cultivate, and harvest. How to encourage growth with both care and intention. How to align planting and harvesting with lunar cycles and planetary movements.

Working magically with cultivation means that every step is taken with awareness. The planting is a ritual, the watering a blessing, and the harvest an act of gratitude.

In traditional magical practice, planting with the waxing Moon encourages growth, while harvesting under the waning Moon enhances potency. The influence of planetary days and hours adds further layers, drawing on the celestial currents that shape the plant's nature. This is not just gardening, it is an act of sacred stewardship in the proper use of the term.

The psychic: building a relationship

Once a plant has been planted, tended, and nurtured, the next stage is to listen. This is the part that modern science ignores, the awareness that plants are sentient in their own way, responding to intention, presence, and thought.

This work involves:

Meditation—sitting with the plant, observing its presence, and listening for its energy.

Dietary interaction—ingesting the plant in teas or tinctures to attune to its essence.

Dream work—placing the plant near the bed or under the pillow to invite visions.

Observation—not just how it grows, but how it moves, what it attracts, and what it repels.

A plant is not just a thing; it is a being with knowledge to share. But it does not speak in words, it speaks in sensation, in imagery, in intuition. To understand it, we must shift our awareness, tuning in to its unique frequency.

This is not about forcing communication; it is about listening.

The astrological: the flow of celestial energies

Every plant carries planetary and elemental energies that shape its nature and influence its effects. Understanding these correspondences allows us to align our work with the greater cosmic forces.

Which planet rules this plant?
Which zodiac sign enhances or balances its energy?
How does the Moon influence its potency?
What elemental forces shape its essence?

This is not just theory, it is a practice of sympatheia, the deep connection between all things.

For example, a plant ruled by Venus will bring harmony and beauty, while one under Mars will carry forceful, protective energy. A herb aligned with Saturn may aid in binding and banishment, while a Lunar plant enhances intuition and psychic vision.

By aligning magical workings with these forces, we enhance the potency of our spells and deepen our understanding of the plant's role in the cosmic web.

The magical: the plant's sigil and name

To work with a plant as an ally, rather than simply a tool, we must understand its magical identity. Every plant has a sigil, a symbolic representation of its spiritual essence. This can be discovered through meditation, divination, or visionary work. A plant's sigil is a key to its deeper mysteries, allowing us to connect with its energy in ritual and spellwork. Likewise, every plant has a Magical Name, not the botanical Latin, not the common folk name, but its true spiritual name which will be unique to the person working with it. This name is often revealed through dream work, trance states, or direct communion with the plant itself. Knowing and using this name deepens the bond, transforming the relationship from one of simple use to one of true collaboration.

With its sigil and name, a plant can be invoked in magical workings even when it is not physically present.

The alchemical: the spagyric essence

At its highest level, alchemy is not just about transforming the plant, it is about transforming ourselves. The act of creating a tincture is more than an extraction of properties; it is an alchemical process of refinement, mirroring the journey of the practitioner. As we separate, purify, and reunite the plant's elements, we undergo the same process within ourselves, breaking down what is unnecessary, distilling what is true, and reintegrating into something greater.

Alchemy teaches us that every material thing has three parts:

The Body (the ash, the fixed essence left after calcination)

The Soul (the essential oil, the extracted essence of the plant)

The Spirit (the volatile spirit, often extracted through fermentation and distillation)

Through the spagyric process, these elements are separated, refined, and brought back together in a more potent and elevated form.

The resulting tincture carries the full power of the plant, not only on a physical level but on an energetic and spiritual level as well.

This is not just herbalism; it is a sacred process, a collaboration between the plant and practitioner, where both are transformed. In working with the Green at this level, we do not simply take from it, we enter a reciprocal relationship, where we grow alongside the plant, learning its mysteries as we refine our own spirit.

Preparations—for the great work

It's often said that the *magnum opus*, the great work, is the labour of a lifetime, not something to be dashed off in a hurry. So, take your time, start slow, and build on solid ground. You will need a bit of equipment, but don't worry, there's no need for full alchemical lab (unless you really want one, in which case, go for it!). What you do need is a patch of earth (or a few pots if space is tight), a watering can, some seeds, and, most importantly, an open and curious mind. Because while the right tools help, the real magic is in the patience, the practice, and the deep listening to the world around you.

To make the tinctures in the way that I make them, you will need a small amount of chemistry kit, which can be bought on the likes of eBay for a very reasonable amount:

i) A mantle heater
ii) A Soxhlet extractor
iii) Various flasks
iv) A pan for burning plant matter.
v) Filter paper and a funnel.
vi) Alcohol and some distilled water.

However, I will also give instructions on how to make the tinctures using the older method. If you use the older method, all you need is jars, and plenty of them.

I recommend that you write a journal or diary of your work so that you can record the information, times, impressions, and teachings you receive when you work directly with the plants in question.

Well, enough of the preamble, let's get going...

PART TWO

THE WORK

CHAPTER FOUR

The growing

First things first, this is not a gardening book. If you're looking for advice on soil pH levels and the best compost, you might want to grab a cup of tea and consult a different tome. What this is, however, is a guide to planting and harvesting herbs in a way that aligns with their nature, and, more importantly, with what you actually want to do with them.

Planting by the Moon

For as long as people have been putting seeds in the ground, they've looked up at the sky for guidance. The idea of planting and harvesting by the Moon isn't some modern New Age trend: it's been around for centuries. Back in ancient Rome, the philosopher Palladius (4th century CE) insisted that all cultivation should be done while the Moon was increasing. Columella (1st century CE) got even more specific, warning that beans had to be planted carefully on the fifteenth day after the New Moon. And if that level of lunar micromanagement wasn't enough, even the *Farmer's Almanac* still gives Moon-based planting advice today.

So why all this fuss about the Moon? Well, it turns out that farmers weren't just making things up for fun. Just like the ocean tides (and the hormones sloshing about in our own bodies), water in the soil and inside plants is affected by the gravitational pull of the Sun and Moon. Seeds absorb the most water during the Full and New Moons, making these times particularly potent for planting.

Over the course of its 28-day cycle, the Moon goes through eight phases, but for our purposes, we only need to focus on four:

New Moon
First Quarter Moon
Full Moon
Third Quarter Moon

For half of the cycle, from New Moon to Full Moon, the Moon is waxing (gaining light). After the Full Moon, it begins to wane (losing light). This cycle isn't just poetic, it has a real effect on how plants grow.

i) Above-Ground Planting

If you're growing something that produces above the ground, you should plant it when the Moon is waxing.

During the New Moon, plant or transplant leafy annuals—lettuce, spinach, cabbage, celery, and their green and leafy friends.

During the First Quarter, focus on plants that produce fruit with external seeds—tomatoes, pumpkins, broccoli, beans, and so on.

ii) Below-Ground (Root) Crops

The waning Moon is your friend if you're after root vegetables or anything that does its best work underground.

Just past the Full Moon, plant root crops and fruit trees—apples, potatoes, beets, turnips, asparagus, and rhubarb all do well at this time.

Put the seed packets down during the Last Quarter (Third Quarter) and step away from the trowel. This is your time to focus on soil maintenance—composting, mulching, weeding, and ensuring your Green allies have the best possible home.

The zodiac and the Moon

Now, if you want to level up your gardening magic, pay attention to the Moon's journey through the zodiac. The Moon moves through all twelve signs in roughly a month, and some signs are far more fertile than others.

Water and Earth signs—Cancer (W), Scorpio (W), Pisces (W), Taurus (E), Virgo (E), and Capricorn (E)—bring moist, fertile conditions. These are the prime times for planting and encouraging healthy growth.

Air and Fire signs—Gemini (A), Libra (A), Aquarius (A), Aries (F), Leo (F), and Sagittarius (F)—are mostly barren. If you plant during these times, don't expect great results unless you're working with particularly hardy or rebellious plants.

This method of lunar and zodiac planting is the approach we'll be using as we work with our plant allies. The following guide is just a rough starting point—I encourage you to experiment, observe, and make your own notes. After all, working with plants is as much about personal experience as it is about tradition.

Astrological Sign	Planting, Harvesting and Other Activities
Aries	Element—Fire
	Plant part—Fruit
	Barren and dry
	Plant climbers, stalks, and fruit trees. Harvest root and fruit for storage.
	Good for pruning and weeding
Taurus	Element—Water
	Plant part—Root
	Productive and moist
	Planting root crops such as potato, mandrake, and dandelion
	Good for transplanting as the earth is accepting
Gemini	Element—Air
	Plant part—Flower
	Barren and dry
	Good for pruning and weeding
Cancer	Element—Water
	Plant part—Leaf
	Productive and moist
	Best sign for all planting and transplanting
Leo	Element—Fire
	Plant part—Fruit
	Very barren and dry
	Best time for pruning and weeding

(Continued)

(Continued)

Astrological Sign	Planting, Harvesting and other activities
Virgo	Element—Earth Plant part—Root Barren and moist Very good for medicinal plants and flowers. Dividing rootstock of perennial flowers in a waning Moon will be successful.
Libra	Element—Air Plant part—Flower Slightly productive Libra would be best Perfumed flowers
Scorpio	Element—Water Plant part—Leaf Very productive and moist Best for plants with poison leaves
Sagittarius	Element—Fire Plant part—Fruit or seed Barren and dry Harvest roots Also, soil preparation works well here
Capricorn	Element—Earth Plant part—Root Productive and dry Suitable for root crop planting and fertilising soil
Aquarius	Element—Air Plant part—Flower Barren and dry Harvest root crops and pest control
Pisces	Element—Water Plant part—Leaf Very productive and moist Second best planting sign

An example:

I want to grow Mullein to help treat my husband's asthma. Now, let's be clear, Mullein will work whether you have a personal relationship with the plant or not. But the difference in effect? Oh, it's huge. Working with a plant you've bonded with is like the difference between getting a generic, lukewarm hug from a distant relative versus a full-on, soul-deep embrace from your best friend.

Mullein, to me, is firmly under the rulership of Saturn. But I'd also place it within Aquarius' domain; its yellow flowers bloom in July, rising like little torch flames, which feels very Aquarian to me. That's not just book knowledge, either; it's something I've intuited through direct work with the plant.

So, when would I plant my Mullein seeds? Ideally, when the Moon is in Aquarius and forming a good aspect with Saturn. I could even take it a step further and check my husband's natal chart to see his personal relationship with Saturn, because why not tailor the magic to him specifically?

When I work with Mullein, it wouldn't just be about planting and harvesting; I'd sit with it and spend time with it, especially on a Saturday (Saturn's day). And when it comes time to make tinctures, I'd do it during a Saturn hour, ideally when Saturn and the Moon are playing nicely together in the sky. Because working in harmony with these planetary energies doesn't just strengthen the medicine, it deepens the whole process, turning it into something truly magical.

The doctrine of signatures, astrology and plants

The doctrine of signatures is described as a method of knowing which plant is applicable for which ailment. It suggests that plants resembling a particular condition or body part can, in some way, treat or alleviate the illness. The walnut, for example, both in its external appearance and its internal effects on the body, is associated with the brain and has been used to treat conditions affecting this organ. Recent research has shown that walnuts aid in the development of over three dozen neurotransmitters essential for normal neurological functioning. The significance of the walnut was well understood in ancient cultures and continues to be used in indigenous healing practices today. Try cracking open a walnut and looking closely—what do you notice?

In ancient Rome, Dioscorides practised medicine and recorded in 65 CE that "The Herb Scorpius resembles the tail of the Scorpion and is good against his biting". Later herbalists and physicians, such as the 12th-century *Physicians of Myddfai* in Wales, as well as Arabic astrologers, incorporated natural sympathies from the ancient world into their medical systems. The Swiss alchemist and physician Paracelsus in the 16th century further popularised the idea that "similar could cure similar", spreading this philosophy across Europe.

In 1684, William Coles declared:

> Though Sin and Sathan have plunged mankinde into an Ocean of Infirmities, yet the mercy of God which is over all his works, maketh Grass to grow upon the Mountains, and Herbs for use of man, and hath not only stamped upon them a distincte form, but also given particular Signatures, whereby man reade, even in legible characters, the use of them.

Some examples of the doctrine include:

A sliced carrot resembles the human eye; the structure of the carrot mirrors the pupil, iris, and radiating lines of the eye. Modern science supports the idea that carrots improve blood supply to the eyes and enhance vision.

Grapes grow in clusters shaped like the heart. Recent research suggests that drinking a glass of red wine each day improves circulation and heart health.

Kidney beans support kidney function and healing; unsurprisingly, they are shaped exactly like human kidneys.

Celery resembles bone structure and contains almost identical concentrations of body salts necessary for maintaining strong bones. The salts in celery help replenish the skeletal system's needs.

Aubergines, avocados, and pears bear a strong resemblance to the uterus and cervix. Research suggests that eating one avocado per week helps balance hormones, shed unwanted birth weight, and prevent cervical cancer.

Personally, I would argue that the doctrine of signatures evolved because specific plants have been in communication with humans. More importantly, humans were given permission by the plants to use them to treat specific conditions and ailments. Do not forget, indigenous peoples tell us plainly: "It was the plant that taught me the remedy".

Plants, astrology, and healing

There has always been a close relationship between plants and astrology, both central to healing practices since the earliest times. In the astrological system, all things on earth fall under the influences, or "sympathies", of one or more planetary powers.

One key astrological tool was the *Decumbiture Chart*, which dates back to the Hellenistic period of the second century BCE. Originally used as an inception chart for diagnosing illness, it was later adapted for medical astrology. The Decumbiture Chart allowed practitioners to determine a disease's nature and likely progression. Herbs were then aligned with astrological correspondences and matched to specific parts of the human body according to the zodiac.

- Aries–Head, Brain, Face
- Taurus–Throat, Neck, Lips
- Gemini–Lungs, Hands, Arms
- Cancer–Stomach, Breasts, Chest, Ribs
- Leo–Heart, Spine, Forearms
- Virgo–Intestines, Lower Spine, Fingers, Spleen
- Libra–Kidneys, Skin, Lumbar Region
- Scorpio–Bladder, Anus, Nose, Appendix
- Sagittarius–Hips, Thighs, Nerves, Arteries
- Capricorn–Knees, Joints, Teeth, Skin
- Aquarius–Legs, Ankles, Circulation of Blood
- Pisces–Feet, Toes, Lymphatic System

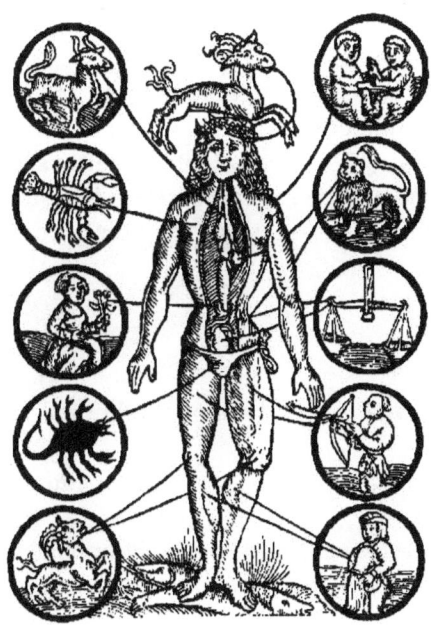

Nicholas Culpeper and the doctrine of correspondences

Nicholas Culpeper, both a botanist and physician, compiled *The English Physician* in 1652, later expanded into *The Complete Herbal* in 1653. This work remains a remarkable cornucopia of pharmaceutical and herbal knowledge from his time. His *Astrological Judgement of Diseases from the Decumbiture of the Sick* (1655) was one of the most comprehensive medical texts of the period and still provides valuable insight into using Decumbiture Charts in medical astrology.

Culpeper studied and classified hundreds of medicinal herbs, aligning them with astrological correspondences that remain relevant to our work today. His observations provide a valuable link between planetary influences and the medicinal properties of plants, a system that continues to be studied and applied in herbal medicine. The following is a summary of Culpeper's astrological plant correspondences.

The Sun

Golden yellow herbs that embody solar energy: Camomile, Celandine, St John's wort.

Tonics and cordials that strengthen the heart, the organ ruled by the Sun: Angelica, Mistletoe, Saffron, Lovage.

Heating herbs that restore vital forces and offer protection against poison: Angelica, Juniper, Rue.

Evergreen herbs, whose constant vitality reflects the steady power of the Sun: Bay Laurel, Juniper, Mistletoe, Pine, Rosemary.

Herbs that enhance vision, since the Sun governs light and sight: Eyebright.

The Moon

Moistening and emollient herbs that soothe and soften: Chickweed, Water Lily.

Cooling, sedating, febrifugal, or anti-inflammatory herbs: Clary Sage, Lettuce, Willow.

Diuretics that cleanse and support the lymphatic system: Cleavers.

Water-dwelling plants that reflect the Moon's element: Water Lily.

Mercury

Carminative herbs that regulate digestion and ease bloating: Caraway, Dill, Fennel, Marjoram, Lavender, Savoury, Southernwood.

Nervine herbs that calm the nervous system and harmonise psychic energy: Lavender, Valerian.

Respiratory tonics that clear the lungs and relieve coughing: Elecampane, Horehound, Liquorice, Mulberry.

Kidney and adrenal gland tonics that regulate and support function: Germander, Lily of the Valley, Parsley.

Many Mercurial herbs are fine, delicate, or umbelliferous, mirroring Mercury's light and agile nature.

Venus

Aromatic herbs with sweet, gentle fragrances: Catnip, Coltsfoot, Cowslip, Feverfew, Groundsel, Mints, Pennyroyal, Meadowsweet, Roses, Thyme, Yarrow.

Culinary spices that enhance flavour and pleasure, such as Fennel and Dill.

Female reproductive tonics that balance menstruation and fertility: Feverfew, Ladies' Mantle, Motherwort, Mugwort, Parsnips, Roses, Vervain, Yarrow.

Kidney and urinary tract herbs that promote healthy function: Artichoke, Burdock, Figwort, Foxglove, Goldenrod, Groundsel, Yarrow.

Mars

Spiny or thorny plants that reflect the combative nature of Mars: Hawthorn, Stinging Nettles, Restharrow, various Thistles.

Strong stimulants, hot and choleric in temperament: Garlic, Onions, Horseradish, Mustard.

Bitter tonics and bile stimulants that aid digestion: Barberry, Blessed Thistle, Gentian, Hops, Wormwood.

Blood-cleansing and fever-reducing herbs that temper the heat of Mars: Madder root.

Wound-healing herbs traditionally used in battle: Plantain.

Jupiter

Liver tonics that aid blood metabolism and humoral balance: Agrimony, Chicory, Dandelion.

Nutritive tonics that fortify vitality and overall constitution: Bilberry, Borage, Chicory, Couchgrass, Dandelion root, Figs.

Warming and digestive stimulants that disperse cold, damp humours: Cinquefoil, Hyssop, Lemon Balm, Sage.

Saturn

Herbs that strengthen bones, joints, and connective tissues: Comfrey, Horsetail.

Astringents that enhance the body's retentive functions: Mullein, Poplar, Shepherd's Purse.

Cooling, bitter purgatives that dispel excess black bile: Fumitory.

Analgesic and narcotic herbs that dull pain: Nightshade, Opium, Wintergreen.

Heavy, grounding herbs that embody Saturn's density and gravity: Comfrey, Solomon's Seal.

Culpeper's work remains a testament to the enduring wisdom of medical astrology and herbal correspondences, linking the celestial and botanical worlds in a system of healing that persists to this day.

As Graeme Tobyn, the author of *Dr Reason and Dr Experience: The English Physician*, states:

> Such correspondences between the elemental and celestial worlds had concerned the human mind since the time of the Pre-Socratic philosophers and of Plato, but it was Paracelsus who first undertook the systematic application of such speculation to a study of Nature. The revival directly inspired Culpeper in mid-seventeenth century England of this approach to promote his synthesis of astrological medicine.[11]

---

[11] Graeme Tobyn, "Dr Reason and Dr Experience: Culpeper's Assignation of Planetary Rulers in The English Physitian," in *From Masha'allah to Kepler: Theory and Practice in Medieval and Renaissance Astrology*, ed. Charles Burnett and Dorian Greenbaum (Lampeter: Sophia Centre Press, 2015).

CHAPTER FIVE

Getting to know you...

One of the hardest things about working with our plant allies is trusting that what you receive from them is real. But then, I would ask—what even is real? How do we define it, and who decides? As with all things, I challenge you to question it for yourself.

Mindset and preparation

The mindset for this work is one of hopeful expectation. For example, you set out with the idea that you will meet a new "Person" and that you and that person will strike up a meaningful conversation, and where both of you will emerge from this interactive experience with well-being. So try the following:

i) Find a plant that speaks to you.
By this, I mean a plant that you see a lot. One that attracts your eye and where you sense that it is following you, almost on purpose. Plants want to work with us, both to make our lives better and to make us understand how we can live together on the planet. We must SEE each other as "humans". Plants will make themselves known to you when you need them, and they will always know what you need.

I will give you a little example. Last year we planted a flowerbed, and when we went to the garden centre, my husband was very attracted to a purple flower with a round head. We bought about four plants and planted them up. During the next few weeks, I often saw my husband veering towards the plants, stroking the flowers, sniffing them, and playing with the leaves. I asked him why he was so attracted to them; he said that he really couldn't explain but that they were "charming flowers". Now, my husband has nothing to do with the craft, and to be honest, he is the type of man who would think this book is ridiculous, but he is also a man who has quite severe asthma, and I had a feeling that the plant was calling to him. So I looked it up in my Culpeper, and this is what he said about Scabious:

Government and virtues

Mercury owns the plant.

Scabious is very effective for all sorts of coughs, shortness of breath, and all other diseases of the breast and lungs, ripening and digesting cold phlegm, and other tough humours, voids them forth by coughing and spitting. It ripens also all sorts of inward ulcers and imposthumes; pleurisy also, if the decoction of the herb dry or green be made in wine, and drank for some time together.

What really made me smile at the time was the realisation that my husband, bless him, with all his asthma troubles, also suffers from stomach complaints and excessive acid. And guess what? Scabious could help with that too! It was one of those moments where the universe just hands you a wink and a nod, confirming that those "intuitive feelings" you get from plants aren't just whimsical daydreams, they're actively at work, all the time.

But here's the funny thing. When drawn to a particular plant, most people feel that initial spark of connection; maybe they pick it up, admire it, and even research it a bit. And then? They move on, get distracted, and carry on as if nothing happened. It's like the plant waves at them, but they're too busy scrolling through life to wave back. So how do we make conscious contact?

Make yourself comfortable

Sitting with the plant in its place of growth is essential. It's like going round their house for a coffee. Go and sit with the plant and just be. Breathe normally and close your eyes and then make room for an experience. This can be anything from feeling their energy, perhaps relating to a particular part of your body. Smelling the plant develops your sense of awareness, and you might perhaps begin to experience a dislocation or displacement. This can sometimes manifest as a non-linear-time shift, as I experienced directly with one particular tree.

When No means NO!

One of the biggest lessons I've learned from working with plants is this: you always know when a plant doesn't want to work with you. No ifs, no buts. In our coven, one of the golden rules is that you never, ever take a wand from a tree that says no. And trust me, that "no" isn't subtle. It's not a polite "Oh, maybe not right now" kind of thing. It's a bodily reaction, one you can't ignore unless you're really determined to bulldoze through the universe's gentle warnings.

In my experience, your body reacts to the plant's energy. A "yes" feels warm, welcoming, like the plant is practically leaning in, excited to work with you. You'll feel lighter, maybe even a little giddy, like an old friend just invited you in for tea.

A "no", on the other hand? Oh, you'll know. It hits you right in the gut and the heart, a sinking, unmistakable sensation. The real question isn't whether you'll notice it, but whether you'll listen.

And that's where things get tricky. As humans, we are terrible at being told "no". We take it personally. We feel entitled because, well, we always have. If we want an apple, we take an apple. If we want a wand, we cut a wand. And when that uneasy, slightly nauseous feeling creeps in as we cut the branch, or our heart suddenly feels heavy, what do we do? We ignore it. Because we want the wand, dammit! And the fancy witch book we just bought says we must have one, and now we've decided this particular branch is the one!

Honestly, we need to get better at listening. The problem with truly listening is that once you've heard, you can't unhear, it becomes real. So if a plant, tree, or spirit gives you a clear "no", honour demands that you respect it. Walk away. No sulking, no throwing a magical tantrum. Don't get too disheartened because another plant will want to work with you. Unfortunately, or rather, fortunately, this one does not.

So, pull up your big witch pants and move on! There's a whole Green World out there waiting for you.

Make a note of what you feel and experience

You might need to go through this process a few times, especially with trees, as they're not exactly known for rushing things.

Once you've spent time with a plant and built a connection, you can respectfully ask what it wants to teach you. Because trust me, if a plant has made itself known to you, it's not just because it fancies the company: it has something to give. The key here is patience. Don't try to force the process; just accept whatever comes through.

You can ask questions, and if you're tuned in, you'll hopefully pick up on what the plant wants to share. You might even ask if there's anything you can do in return. Does it need extra care? A different environment? Some plants will tell you what they need straight up. And yes, sometimes that means ... urine.

Now, I know what you're thinking, Did she just say the plant might ask for wee? Yes, I did. And before you wrinkle your nose, let me remind you: urine is an excellent source of nitrates, which plants use to make proteins. Plus, it creates a tangible energetic link between you and the plant. But let's be smart about this, public urination is still frowned upon in most civilised societies. Instead of getting yourself arrested, you can always collect your offering in a jar and then pour it discreetly onto your plant. A little witchy cunning goes a long way.

Once your relationship with the plant deepens, you can ask it for its name and sigil. This is a remarkable and deeply personal connection, and when a plant shares this with you, you know you've genuinely been accepted into its world.

Plant names and their associations

In my experience, the names that plants give you are tied to their smell. That's their signature, their unique essence. The problem? Well, plant scents don't exactly translate into pronounceable human words unless you fancy trying to communicate in a series of sniffs and pheromonal impressions. So, the plant and I have to reach a mutual agreement, a sort of linguistic compromise on what we'll use to talk to each other.

A plant will nudge your subconscious to provide either a name or a sigil. If you get a sigil, fantastic! That's a ready-made key, a two-dimensional symbol that can be used just like any other sigil, a gateway into the plant's astral presence. If you receive a name, however, I'd strongly recommend turning that into a sigil as well, to give yourself a direct link to the plant's deeper reality.

A note on "Faces"

One of the things we've discovered when working with a plant as a group is that each person might receive a different name or sigil for the same plant. This often leads to the inevitable question: Doesn't that mean it's all just in our heads?

Not at all! And here's how I explain it to my coven:

I am Sian. To my husband, I am Siany—his loving, supportive wife … unless he's done something idiotic, in which case, I become a homicidal and psychotic entity.

To my daughter, Cerys, I am Mam—cuddly, sometimes scary when she's misbehaved, and full of unconditional love. In her mind, I have never had sex, because that would mean Mam and Dad did that, and eww.

To my coven, I am their leader, strict but caring, a guide through the magical world.

To my karate students, I am Sabom, the slightly unhinged, masochistic instructor who enjoys pushing them to their limits.

See? Same person, different faces, depending on who's looking at me and what kind of relationship we have. Plants are exactly the same. They reveal themselves to you based on your connection with them. So, if someone else in the group receives a different name or sigil for the same plant, it doesn't mean one of you is wrong—it means you're each seeing the face of the plant that is most relevant to you.

And that, in my book, is proof of just how real and personal these relationships truly are.

Doorway plants

Mugwort was my first doorway plant. She was gentle, kind, and wild, and when I first started working with her, I was deep in the throes of menopause, which inevitably shaped our relationship. As a Venusian plant with strong lunar ties, she held the energy of the Moon, while I was at a point where my own Moon cycle was coming to an end. She helped me untangle the idea that losing my menstrual cycle meant losing my womanhood and sexuality, guiding me to see that these things run far deeper than blood and biology.

One of my coveners, however, had an entirely different experience. For her, Mugwort was sexually electrifying, awakening a sense of freedom and excitement in her own body. Where I found gentle reassurance, she found wild liberation. Mugwort showed her that fertility and sexuality were not just about reproduction, but about power, pleasure, and personal sovereignty.

And that is really the heart of what I am saying here. A plant will build a relationship with you, but that relationship will be shaped by you, your body, your mind, your emotions, and whatever you bring to the experience. The magic is not just in the plant, but in the dance between the two of you.

On forming a closer relationship

One of the methods of forming closer relationships with plants is to grow the plant from seed in your own garden. This is a beautiful way of bonding with your plant right from the start.

You can obtain seeds for most medicinal plants, or wild plants can be bought from reputable seed sellers like Jekka's Herbs. Or you can just go out into the wild and forage for seeds when they come into season. I like this last method as it gives you a starting point with the mother plant. However, you must form a relationship with that plant before removing its seeds, so:

a) Take your plant seed home and start meditating with it. My advice here is to start by working meditatively with the plant, and if it is safe to do so, try dieting the plant before seeking any information from outside sources. This way, your impressions will be entirely your own, free from outside influence.

b) Write down everything you experience—every feeling, every image, every whisper of insight. Let the plant speak to you first. You should only begin looking into the plant's astrological and mythological associations after this initial work. That way, you build a relationship based on your own lived experience rather than colouring it with someone else's interpretations.

c) Look at its astrological correspondence using the Culpeper method, but also, don't forget to trust your instincts on this and try to time your meditations with those more auspicious times.

d) Plant your seed in line with the Moon correspondences. You could even perform a ritual to make the planting a more spiritual act.
e) After that, you can water the plant, talk to it, and encourage it to sprout and grow, all the time listening to the plant speak in their way to you.

A word of warning, once you start working with a plant like this, you are basically adopting a very enthusiastic, leafy lodger. The bond you form is powerful, and before you know it, your garden will be absolutely teeming with the stuff. It is lovely, of course, but let's just say my husband has had more than a few words to say about the ever-expanding Mugwort Empire.

Plant tribes and plant individuals

I have found that when I build a relationship with a particular plant, it is like being introduced to its extended family, the group mind or tribe mind of that species. Befriend Mugwort, for example, and suddenly Mugworts everywhere will start waving at you from roadside verges, popping up in unexpected places, and generally making their presence very well known.

However, this does not mean you have free rein to go snipping bits off any old plant just because you have had a nice chat with one of its cousins. Yes, plants are part of a tribe mind, but they are also individuals. The Mugwort in my garden knows me well, and when I harvest from her, I do so with respect and gratitude. I use everything I take, and anything left over is returned as an offering.

Now, if I am walking in my local area, the plants there recognise me, and we have a level of mutual understanding. But step outside my usual stomping ground, and things shift. The plants further afield do not know me as well, and strolling up to a Mugwort in the country park and lopping off a chunk just because it is looking particularly lush is, quite frankly, rude. Not only will this disturb the plant itself, but you might also upset the wider collective mind, and that can have consequences for your relationships with your own Green allies.

I am not saying never wild harvest, just do it properly. Ask permission first, wait for an answer, and, most importantly, respect the plant's decision. Nobody likes an uninvited guest who helps themselves to the best bits without so much as a hello.

Dieting the plant

We can see from the practice of indigenous peoples that dieting a plant is an excellent way to contact the plant spirit. However, to do this without killing yourself, you need to be sure that the plant is not poisonous and does not have a detrimental effect on your health, especially true if you suffer from any ongoing medical conditions. An example would be eating foxgloves when you have a heart condition: not a good plan unless you have a fetish for doctors. You can diet your plant in quite a few ways.

a) *Make a tea*–using a fresh or dried herb, you can make tea with boiling water and drink it before your meditation.
b) *Eating the plant*–many plants are bitter to the taste, so this is not one I would recommend.
c) *Smelling the plant*–when sitting out with your plant, you can crush up leaves and hold them up in the cup of your hand and smell them. This is great for aromatic plants like Rosemary and Lavender, but all plants have an individual smell. Get to know that smell, and you will begin to know that plant.
d) *Make an essence*–use blessed water and stand the live plant's leaves in the water during sunlight hours. Then dilute the solution by at least one hundred and use a drop on the tongue. This method is how Bach Flower Remedies are made.
e) *The Herb pillow*–put fresh herbs into a bag and put it in your pillowcase. This allows the plant to communicate with you in dreams and is a fantastic way to know the plant.

A quick note on poisonous plants

What do you do if your plant is poisonous? Use your common sense—**do not eat it!** Honestly, it should go without saying, but let's just make it absolutely clear: if your plant has a reputation for being lethal, do not turn yourself into a test subject.

Instead, use a sit-with technique. Spend time near the plant, observe it, connect with it energetically, and ask it how best to build a relationship. Some plants will communicate through dreams, others through subtle shifts in your awareness. Let the plant guide the process rather than rushing in with a teacup and a death wish.

Do your research. Find out what the lethal dose is—if one exists—and whether the plant has been safely used in any capacity before. Some plants that are considered dangerous in large quantities have been used historically in carefully controlled ways. One of the most valuable books I have ever found was a pre-1940 British Pharmacopeia (the older, the better). These gems hold recipes for teas, oils, unguents, and creams that were once used to improve health and treat various ailments.

For example, I turned to my trusty 1930s edition when I wanted to learn how to make a non-lethal milk of the poppy. And that is the key: knowledge and respect. Approach with care, do your homework, and never assume that just because a plant can be used, it should be, especially not without knowing exactly what you are doing.

CHAPTER SIX

Simple alchemical praxis

In his book *The Practical Handbook of Plant Alchemy* (1985), Manfred M. Junius states that spagyric plant remedies differ from non-spagyric ones because the plant is "opened up" and by its own process "liberates stronger curative powers".[12]

Plant alchemy involves both practical and spiritual work. We observe that the corporeal and incorporeal aspects of the plant are termed alchemically the *tria prima*. The *tria prima* represents what we call the plant's Sulphur, Mercury, and Salt. These we then separate and recombine (the motto: *solve et coagula*), so that after several stages and processes, the plant is exalted to its highest state.

You might ask why we use terms such as *Salt* but this represents the plant's body; *Mercury* represents the plant's spirit (or mind); and *Sulphur* represents the plant's soul. So, in the physical realm, Salt (body) is the plant's leaves, flowers, and roots. Mercury (spirit/mind) is the alcohol from the distillation of the plant matter; on occasion, this can even be types of water. Sulphur (soul) is the essential oil of the plant.

---

[12] Manfred M. Junius, *The Practical Handbook of Plant Alchemy: An Herbalist's Guide to Preparing Medicinal Essences, Tinctures, and Elixirs* (Rochester, VT: Inner Traditions, 1985). https://www.simonandschuster.com/books/Spagyrics/Manfred-M-Junius/9781594771798.

Remember I said earlier that the smell of the plant is its name. In alchemical terms, the perfume you get when you purify a plant's essential oil is its soul or its personality. So, for example, when you smell a plant, it is actually showing you, or better revealing to you, its soul.

To work alchemically with our plant friends, you will also need a basic understanding of astrology. I work by looking at the closest astrological match that would work with the plant, e.g. when working with Mugwort I look for a good aspect between Venus and the Moon. Ideally, I would like Venus in Taurus and the Moon in Cancer, but this is a particular astrological condition that is very rare, so in this case I would try for the Moon in Taurus or Cancer as these have an excellent aspect to Venus.

In this respect, I try to choose a Venus hour at the correct time, then place my Mugwort in a thimble and place it within my Soxhlet apparatus (see below for the process). I would then draw its sigil on the side of the Soxhlet glass. In this particular case, and this is an important aspect to my work, I would involve an invocation to Hekate. I would ask Hekate to create a bridge between the spirit of the plant and my own spirit. Then, and by using this link, it can assist in the spiritual, psychic, and overall production of a powerful medicinal tincture from my plant. I would also recite the *Orphic Hymn to Venus* and then recite the *Orphic Hymn to the Moon*—again, these are particularly to be used with *Mugwort*. I tend to use Thomas Taylor's translations, purely for their poetic delicacy.

I would then run distilled vodka (as close to 100% as I can make it) through the Soxhlet for as many circulations as I can obtain in the planetary hour. Working in this way, you will discover, is a very meditative experience. For when one watches the alcohol circulate and take on the plant's spirit, it is truly beautiful. I recommend that you observe this operation respectfully, that is, with mindfulness, producing a deep understanding involving the co-operation between you and the plant. Ideally, praxis must be undertaken with focused concentration and a sense of gratitude and love. Now, as you watch, try quietly saying its name or drawing its sigil on a piece of paper, and then meditate and project the volatile nature of the plant's *energeia* into the circulation as it proceeds—this will be explained more fully below.

Old style tincturing

In this method, begin by cleaning a jar. I know you all have them: show me a witch and I will show you a house full of pots. Use a form of alcohol. Brandy is the traditional alcohol of choice for many alchemists, but I use vodka purely because I want the taste and smell of the plant to come through rather than the taste and aroma of the brandy itself. For this reason, I have to distil my vodka from the standard 70% proof to as close to 90% as I can, using a standard distillation apparatus.

You will need a clean cloth to wrap your jar in after you start your tincture.

A warm place is needed for your tincture to ferment. Try to make it easy to access, as you will need to shake it regularly.

I like to use this form of tincturing for delicate plants, which are less suitable for the Soxhlet process. I have used this old style tincturing process for Poppy and Rose.

Soxhlet tincturing

This is an excellent tincture method, which will allow you to create a tincture in a very short time. It also allows you to use very fresh herbs and will give excellent tincture results. To do this type of tincturing, you need apparatus that costs money, however. I have found that eBay provides an excellent source of equipment.

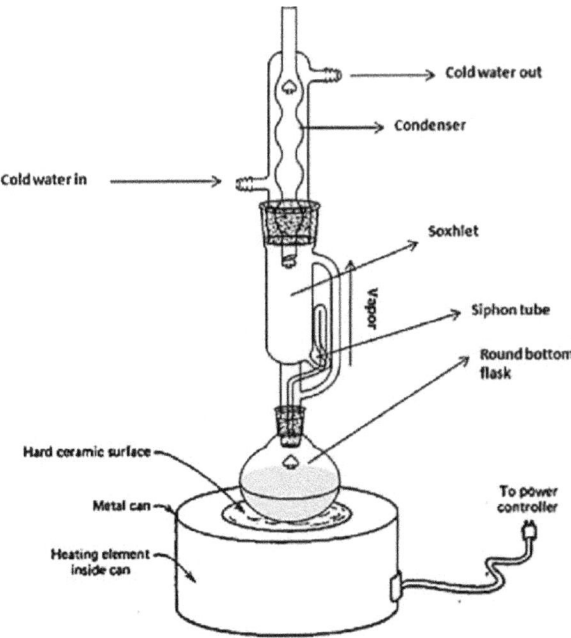

Figure 2. Full Soxhlet set up.

A. How it works

1. Place your thimble packed with your herb into the Soxhlet. For this, I use cotton tea bags and stuff the bag with as much herb as I can.
2. Place the condenser into the top of the Soxhlet and then run cold water through the pipes attached to the water in and water out attachments; make sure that these are always in a bucket, or it makes for a messy day. I use a fishpond pump and tubing through a bucket of iced water, attached to the condenser in, to circulate the water out.
3. Place your alcohol, previously distilled, into the flask in the heater.
4. Bring the heater slowly to the boiling point of the alcohol, which is around 80 degrees—your entire system is enclosed, so do this slowly. You can place a thermometer at the top of the apparatus.
5. Watch and observe.

B. Combining the body and the spirit

1. After your circulation, remove your plant body from the thimble and burn it to ash in a clean dish. Do not use ceramic dishes for this: I once lost a body that I had been working on for about a month doing this. Sadly it must be a metal type dish.
2. Wash the remaining ashes with distilled water and evaporate them off.
3. Repeat this until you are left with a white ash. Don't be surprised that there will be very little of this left in your dish.
4. Swill the white ash out of the dish with your tincture.
5. This results in a combination of the spirit and body of the plant. This can also be done by imbibing by pipette the spirit back into the plant as you are heating it.

My own personal alchemical and spagyric equipment

For my own tincturing process see Figs. 2 to 4, where I demonstrate the stages involved in the circulations (*circulatoria*) using the Soxhlet condenser:

Stage 1

The herb thimble positioned in the Soxhlet—note the sigil on the Soxhlet and the heating mantle or flask. The thimble I use is a reusable tea bag made from cotton. The alcohol is placed in a flask, which is then placed in the heating mantle. I use 250ml of vodka for this.

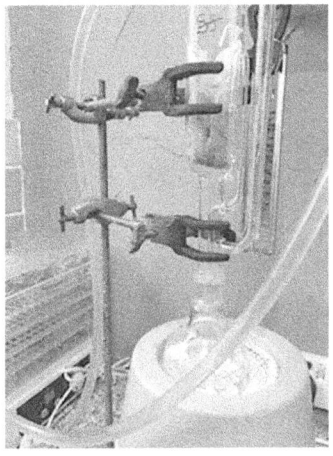

Figure 3.

Stage 2

The circulations begin.

This is the bit where you say, "Look at the colour on that".

Circulation (*circulatoria*) occurs for the whole planetary hour.

Figure 4.

Stage 3

Completion of the extraction phase.

Once your circulations have finished, place the tincture into a bottle and remember that the remains of the plant are still sacred, as your 'body' remains after death.

Figure 5.

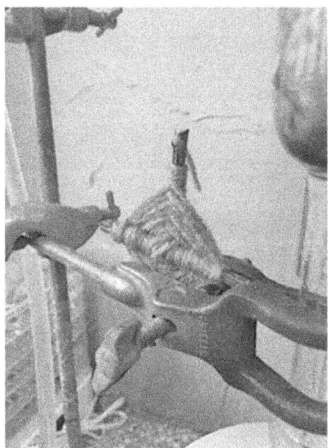

Figure 6. Details of a little talisman that I made out of Mugwort stalks that have been made into an offering.

Figure 7. Shows the ash before washing.

On producing your final spagyric tincture

If you run out of time in your planetary hour's work, then I advise that you respectfully store it and then wait for the commencement of the next planetary hour.

Now place the plant remains in a flame-resistant pan and, along with any fresh or dried plant that you might have left over, let it now burn down to ash.

The ash will be black, so you can wash it with distilled water and by putting the solution through a filter paper and then simply evaporating the water afterwards.

Repeat this process: the ash will first turn from black to grey, but keep going until it turns to a pure white. You won't get much, but don't let that worry you.

Now, mix the white ash back into the tincture, where you will have now produced a spagyric medicine–the purified plant body, spirit, and soul are now recombined/reunited (*solve leads to coagula*) in a more exalted state.

CHAPTER SEVEN

Making your practice magical

To create anything magical, you need to learn how to tap into and activate a particular state of mind. It's not just about ritual performance; it's about engaging your mind's eye through desire and will. When these elements work together, properly directed, they bring about the magical outcome you seek.

The role of Hekate in my plant work

For me, Hekate stands at the heart of working with Green Magic. She is the weaver of my connection with the Green People, the one who guides and deepens my relationship with them. Few deities are as vast, as boundless, as she is. Hekate moves through the sky, the earth, the underworld, and the sea; she stands at the crossroads of life and death, of doorways and birth. Yet what many overlook is her presence within the Green World itself. She is not just a goddess of thresholds and transitions, she is a goddess of the living earth, the soil, and all that grows from it.

Her many names whisper of this truth. Zootrophia, the Nourisher of Life. Reskicthon, she who bursts forth from the earth. Hekate Chthonia, Queen of the soil beneath our feet. She moves in harmony with Kore, the Maiden of the Fields, threading herself through the cycles of life, death, and rebirth. Through these names and their power, Hekate holds dominion over the plant kingdom, her authority woven into every root and leaf.

I have found that calling upon Hekate is especially powerful when seeking to connect with a plant ally. She is the bridge, the guide, the force that amplifies and refines the link between human and Green. Her aspect as Polymorphos, the Many-Formed, reveals her as a goddess of all things, shifting and shaping herself through countless forms, binding together the worlds of spirit and matter.

To invoke her is to invite transformation, to open yourself to the language of the Green, to listen beyond words, and to let her presence guide you into deeper communion with the living world.

A short ritual for contacting the spirit of the place (genius loci) and your plant ally

Perform on a new Moon or when the Moon is waxing: if possible, when Mercury is in a good aspect to the Moon or when the Moon is waxing in Gemini.

Go out into the wood or your place of choice; this can be anywhere that is special to you.

Safety first: make sure that you are not disturbed; people tend to look askance at someone in full robes in the middle of nowhere, so be subtle; jeans and a jumper are sometimes a better option.

Standing in the area where you are to do the work, sound the following with confidence:

Hekas Hekas Este Bebeloi (a transliteration of the Greek, and a translation in English means: "Afar, Afar, be ye all profane"). You can, if you wish, simply use the English.

Now, visualise yourself within the enclave of your aura. See it as a shield against any harm, but know that you are safe within and that you are prepared to welcome in those powers and energies. Please note that we do not use a circle in this ritual, for we *want* the spirits to come in, and if we created a traditional magic circle, this would be a barrier against the spirits we want to attract. However if you are uncomfortable with this approach, then please adapt and use a circle of your own choice, but understand that your contact may be limited and the results not as powerful as one might expect.

Invocation to Hekate

"Mother of the form around me,
Life and death in one deep breath.
Universal heart's compassion, Mother of both birth and death.
Cup and womb of power indwelling,
Give to me the kingdom's key,
Shadow to the light's great power, Mother of the world to be.
Scythed one standing on the crossroad
In between the dark and light,
Give to me an ancient power,
Grant to me the ancient sight.
Hekate of the green, Zootrophia, Chthonia,
I ask you to be a bridge between myself and the spirit who dwells in this place.
Be a doorway through which I may pass into understanding,
Make communication easy and let us form a bond."

A Call to the "Spirit of the Place"

"Spirits, guardians of this place,
In this time and in this place
I call to you,
Come, for I would know you better
Come and let me learn from you
Spirit of the trees and plants
I ask you to bless this work and give me your aid.
I come with an open heart and with good intent."

The offering

The offering can be either incense, tea, or alcohol; otherwise, do some of your own research about your place of choice, and then make a specific offering to the types of spirits that you hope to work with. For example, if you are in a wooded area then urine is an excellent offering as it has lots of "love nitrates" in it for plants to use as food. Just take care that you don't offend anyone in the vicinity!

Open your heart centre and put the "call" out When the *genius loci* or plant spirit of the place comes, you will undoubtedly feel its presence. Do not expect to understand it immediately, but just let your intuition work. Make sure you remember exactly what the feeling was, especially when you come to document the whole experience in your magical diary or journal.

Meditational praxis

I always make a meditational "trip" to meet the plant spirit in question. The spirit will then take on a form that will speak to you and to you alone (remember the notion of different masks).

A personal meditational experience with Mugwort

Sitting in a wood, I close my eyes and take three deep breaths; I relax my body from the head down to my feet, and I feel a movement from here to there. I open my eyes, and I am sitting in a garden. It's not a tidy place: plants are growing wildly, and the feeling I have is one of uncoordinated growth and competition. It feels blocked, each plant limiting the other to such an extent that I cannot tell which plant is which. There is a space in the middle where no plants grow; it is a circle of gritty earth, and from the soil starts to rise a plant. She grows very quickly, higher and higher until she is about three feet tall. Her leaves are green, but as the breeze catches them, I see the silver flash of the underside. She waves back and forth in the wind. As I watch, her movement entrances me, and her swaying rhythm is both hypnotic and contagious. I now start to sway in time. As I bend to and fro with the plant, it changes, and a small woman with hands in the air is rocking in front of me.

She is dressed in green, with silver hair and silver eyes. She bends, and as she does so, she takes my hands, and I begin to dance. As I spin and sway her smell enters me, and with it, her name. As I turn, I see the untidy growth of plants around change and become well ordered. Each plant has the best place, and each plant allows me to see it for the first time.

Many of them are utterly unknown to me, but they shine in such a way that makes them more apparent. The veil that the Green People wear now lifts, and my eyes clear. I can now perceive a new reality, one where the plants see me and acknowledge my existence. The smell is overwhelming now, and it enters my body; speaking its name loudly, I can see a sigil forming in the air. It shines in a silver and green sheen. I dance and spin, feeling dizzier and dizzier, until I fall to the ground, and then looking up, I see the plant once again but this time in the place of the dancer. She continues to wave as I know she will continue to wave to me wherever I go. She sees me. I close my eyes, but the feeling of completeness and joy, and the smell follow me back to my seat by the Mugwort. Her leaves now brush against me, and her odour now wafts gently through the afternoon breeze. I leave my offering and speak her name aloud. I thank her for the honour she has bestowed on me. As I go home, I sense that I have left a bit of myself in the wood, but gained something more magical and equally as wonderful.

Making a sigil for your plant ally

Simple method: say the name over and over quietly like a mantra, preferably while sitting with the actual plant, then wait patiently for an image to form. Draw the image and then use it as your sigil for the plant.

A more complex method involves you researching a plant from Culpeper and then which planet is associated with the plant. You can then create a planetary *Kamea* (a magic square) from which you can trace out a sigil based on its name.

How to make and use a planetary square

Planetary squares are based on the theosophic extension of the number traditionally associated with the planet. Each line of the square must add up to that extended number, for example Saturn uses a 3 x 3 square:

4	9	2
3	5	7
8	1	6

The Saturn square

The traditional planetary number for Saturn is 3. This is based on the Kabbalistic attribution and study of the Tree of Life, and where Saturn is assigned to the third Sephira (*Binah* in Hebrew). Thus, by Theosophic extension, the 3 results in a 3 x 3 square. This means that in all directions on the Kamea the numbers will add up to 15, or all the numbers in the complete square will add up to 45. Thus, and by the extension/reduction of 15 = 1 + 5 = 6, which is added to the 3 for Saturn we get 9. Also by adding all the numbers in the square from 1 to 9 = 45 we get by reduction 4 + 5 = 9. The number 9 result is important and allows us to create the squares needed for the kamea on which the sigil can be traced. Furthermore, the divine names associated with Saturn all have numerological values of 3, 9, or 15. The names of the intelligence of Saturn and the spirit of Saturn have a value of 45. These values are calculated by writing out the names in Hebrew and then adding up the value of each included letter, as each Hebrew letter can represent both a sound and a numerical value.

When I started to use the psychic sigil method, my personal doubt demon yet again emerged, and I was never wholly convinced that the sigil I had obtained from my Mugwort was its actual sigil. I honestly believed it was my mind that was giving me exactly what I wanted. I had never completed or seen a traditional Kamea sigil for that plant. However, when I did make the psychic connection, it bore a striking resemblance to the sigil that I had received. To say I was extremely excited by this synchronicity would be an understatement. So I then rushed out into the garden to tell my Mugwort. I was received by what can only be described as a plant version of "Really … Really … still with this!" said in something of an exasperated Mugwort tone. This, as they say, taught me an invaluable lesson, and one that I have never forgotten.

Once you have your sigil, you can engage in more psychic and spiritual investigations of your chosen plant. You can use the sigil as an interstitial doorway in order to pass through the veil and into that of a more meditative and "hidden" space. In here, you will experience the plant spirit, and then by working together you can establish further medicinal, spiritual relationship, and a deeper psychic connection. As a result, you will create a permanent anchor for your overall practice with your plant. An even more magical occurrence is that you will be able to work with that plant spirit even if it's in the middle of winter and your plant remains dormant underneath the earth.

Obtaining a sigil is therefore one of the most magical works you will perform, because it provides a most beautiful and patient form of learning experience initiated by both you and the plant. So persevere in this magical work, for indeed it will prove to be worth it in the end.

PART THREE

THE PLANTS

A M - I S - R E L

THE
MUGWORT

Mugwort

Culpeper on Mugwort

Common Mugwort hath divers leaves lying upon the ground, very much divided, or cut deeply in about the brims, somewhat like wormwood, but much larger, of a dark green colour on the upper side, and very hoary white underneath. The stalks rise to be four or five feet high, having on it such like leaves as those below, but somewhat smaller, branching forth very much towards the top, whereon are set very small, pale, yellowish flowers like buttons, which fall away, and after them come small seeds, in closed in round heads. The root is long and hard, with many small fibres growing from it, whereby it takes strong hold on the ground; but both stalks and leaves do lie down every year, and the root shoots anew in the Spring. The whole plant is of a reasonable scent, and is more easily propagated by the slips than the seed.

Time

It flowers and seeds in the end of summer.

Government and virtues

This is an herb of Venus, therefore maintains the parts of the body she rules, remedies the diseases of the parts that are under her signs, Taurus and Libra. Mugwort is with good success put among other herbs that are boiled for women to apply the hot decoction to draw down their courses, to help the delivery of the birth, and expel the after-birth. As also for the obstructions and inflammations of the mother. It breaks the stone, and opens the urinary passages where they are stopped. The juice thereof made up with Myrrh, and put under as a pessary, works the same effects, and so does the root also. Being made up with hog's grease into an ointment, it takes away wens and hard knots and kernels that grow about the neck and throat, and eases the pains about the neck more effectually, if some field daises be put with it. The herb itself being fresh, or the juice thereof taken, is a special remedy upon the overmuch taking of opium. Three drams of the powder of the dried leaves taken in wine is a speedy and the best certain help for the sciatica. A decoction thereof made with Camomile and Agrimony, and the place bathed therewith while it is warm, takes away the pains of the sinews, and the cramp.

Mythology and folklore

Venus is the planet of love but not the physical love that we come to associate with it. Venus is about love in all its forms. It is the love of family, love of home, love of country, love of the land, love of self and love of the other. When working with Mugwort you can see that she is a Herb of Venus and the Moon. This is because when you look at the leaf you see the Green of Venus on the front of the leaf, whilst hidden at the back you see the silver of the Moon.

Mugwort has a two-fold nature. In the Venus aspect, it is a herb of the blood; it clears out the womb both during menstruation and as a herb that aids in the delivery of children.

In the *Physicians of Myddfai*, if a child is found to have died in the womb, Mugwort is tied to the inner thigh, and the child will be delivered very soon after; however, the Mugwort must be removed or haemorrhaging is probable. It has been used for many years as a uterine cleanser to combat sterility and as an abortifacient.

In its Moon aspect she is a dreaming plant; she opens the doors to remembering dreams and deepens the trance in meditation. It is this aspect that is most useful to the witch. Mugwort is a plant that assists in beginning to work with other plants. She is kind and gentle and allows you to make mistakes whilst guiding you to communicate with her. She is vibrant and happy to work with you, and once you make contact, she will find you wherever you go. My house is full of Mugwort: my drive, my garden, and my road. All now festooned with Mugwort where none had existed before my communion with this unique plant.

The tales of Mugwort

Mugwort is an Old Herb. In the ancient *Nine Herbs Charm* from the Norse Tradition we find:

The Lay of the Nine Herbs

Be mindful, Mugwort, what you revealed,
What you established at the great proclamation.
Una you are called, oldest of herbs, you are
strong against three and against thirty, you are strong
against poison and against onfliers [flying venoms]
you are strong against the foe who goes through the land.

And you, Waybroad [Plantain], mother of herbs,
open from the east, mighty within. Over you
chariots creaked, over you queens rode, over you
brides cried out, over you bulls snorted.
All this you withstood, and confounded.
So you withstand poison and flying venom, and
the foe who goes through the land.

Stune this herb is called, she grew on a stone, she
stands against poison, she attacks pain.
Stithe [hard] she is called, she confounds poison, she
drives out evils, she casts out poison.
This is the herb that fought against the worm,
this is strong against poison, she is strong against flying venoms,
she is strong against the foe who goes through the land.

> Rout you now, Attorlathe [Venomloather], the less the
> more, the more the less until there be a remedy for him
> against both.
>
> Remember you, Maythe [Camomile], what you revealed,
> what you accomplished at Alorford,
> that never for flying venom did he yield life since
> for him a man prepared Maythe for food.
>
> This is the herb that is called Wergule.
> This a seal sent over the sea ridges, as a
> remedy against the harm of another poison.

All varieties of Artemesia (another name for Mugwort) are sacred to the Goddess Artemis, lady of the Moon, who gives comfort (or death) to women in labour, as well as blessings on the hunt, and fertility. Mugwort is also tied to Artemis/Diana and Hekate, patron of herbalists and midwives. There is evidence of Mugwort in ancient Egypt, where the smoke was an offering to Isis. Mugwort has roots that pre-date modern written history, so not all its ancient past is that well known.

Roman soldiers are said to have put Mugwort in their sandals to stop their feet from getting tired, and Mugwort is well known as an herb for any wandering soul. The great Roman herbalist, Pliny the Elder, said of Mugwort, "The wayfaring man that hath the herb tied about him feeleth no weariness at all and he can never be hurt by any poisonous medicine, by any wild beast, neither yet by the sun itself. A very impressive testament to this hardy herb. Mugwort is said not only to protect, but to reverse hexes, and if hidden near doorways, it will stop unwelcome visitors."

Magical uses of Mugwort

To make a tea, infuse one cup of hot (not boiling) water with at least two teaspoons of dried herbs or three to five teaspoons of fresh herbs, with honey. Leave for about five to ten minutes to allow infusion.

Mugwort is also excellent for working dream magic, for scrying and divination, and also as a sweep or wash for cleansing negativity from spaces. When smoked she gives you a sense of euphoria and clarifies the meditational vision.

Using Mugwort juice to aid in skrying

Cut fresh Mugwort when the Moon is in a good aspect to Venus, using a pestle and mortar or a juicer if you want to be modern. Crush the Mugwort and rub the juice over the crystal or mirror that you are going to skry in. When you are ready to start the skrying process, put a small amount of the juice over your eyelids, and ask the Mugwort spirit to act as a link between you and the spirit you are skrying for.

Medical uses for Mugwort

Mugwort may be used as a digestive tonic combatting worms in a similar if more gentle way than Wormwood. It is also an excellent antidepressant and relaxant, so it can be used to calm nerves and give a general sense of wellbeing.

But its main fame as a medicinal herb is in female reproductive health. Mugwort can affect a toning and a stimulating effect on the uterus. It helps in irregular periods and helps in the expulsions of the placenta.

Taking tea as a menstrual aid is suggested; however, there is a contradiction that if you are pregnant, Mugwort can hasten labour.

Dose

Infusion of dried herb 0.5g–2g. Use three times daily.

Personal observations from practice

Mugwort is therefore a child of Venus. She is approachable, friendly, and almost eager to work with you.

She wants to be in your world; yes, you can work with her with great success when the Moon is in Taurus or Virgo, but I also think there is an incredible place for working with her when Venus is in Cancer, or when the Moon is in Taurus or Virgo. Here, her role as a door opener and a dream giver is tied to the Moon, and she is a beautiful starting point for anyone initiating this type of work. When working with Mugwort, I have learned about the feeling of freedom, the joy of growth unfettered by worries, and, as I have demonstrated, she was the door for my first forays into the Green. As a result, I have a special love for her spirit.

Please note, there is no entry in Charubel's work for Mugwort.

Modern research on Mugwort

Mugwort (Artemisia vulgaris) has been getting some attention in modern pharmaceutical research, and while we are a long way from it being the next big thing in mainstream medicine, the studies so far are rather interesting. Scientists have found that it has a fair few useful properties; it has been shown to have antioxidant, antibacterial, antifungal, and even pain-relieving effects. There is also research suggesting it could help protect the liver, ease muscle spasms, and have some oestrogenic activity, which might explain why it has been used traditionally for menstrual health. All of this comes down to its complex mix of essential oils, flavonoids, and sesquiterpene lactones.

Mugwort has a long history of medicinal use across different cultures, and even today you will find it promoted for digestive issues, irregular periods, and even high blood pressure. It has also been used as a sedative, laxative, and liver tonic, and some folk swear by it for calming irritated skin, particularly in cases of severe burns and scars. One of the better known uses of Mugwort is in traditional Chinese medicine, where it plays a starring role in moxibustion, a practice that involves burning the herb near the skin to promote healing. Some studies suggest this can have effects on the nervous system, and may even help turn breech babies by encouraging foetal movement. It has also been used for menstrual cramps and digestive issues.

Now, a word of caution: Mugwort is not for everyone. Some people have allergic reactions to it, especially if they are sensitive to ragweed and similar plants. It can cause sneezing, sinus issues, and even contact dermatitis in some unlucky folk. Most importantly, if you are pregnant, stay away from it. Mugwort has been known to stimulate menstruation and could potentially trigger contractions, so best not take the risk.

Creating an alchemical tincture

Make the tincture on a day when Venus is in good aspect to the Moon and preferably either Venus or the Moon is in Cancer or Taurus.

The plant name I received is Amisrel.

There is no Charubel name or sigil for this plant.

Personal Sigil

Venus Kamea

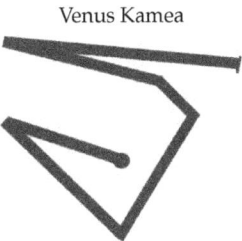

Dieting the plant

Mugwort can be drunk in a tea, smoked, and made into a wine infusion, which is a beautiful way of taking the herb. It is a pretty bitter herb to eat, so a tea or wine infusion is the best way to go. When smoking herbs to make relationships, do not combine this with other practices or you will obtain a confused or mixed picture of the herb's effect. Don't use tobacco; my recommendation is that you should use a pipe. Then there is also the bonus of looking like a mad Gandalf to your friends.

Meditation

She came to me as a lithe green woman, silver hair flowing like mist, silver eyes gleaming with secrets. She did not speak in words, but in movement, swaying and spinning, wild and free. I mirrored her dance, and in that rhythm, we understood one another.

She was untamed, a creature of a time before humankind, carrying the pulse of the earth before it knew our footsteps. She showed me rivers the colour of blood, and I knew this was the path of blood magic and medicine, the work she would guide me through. Her energy coiled deep in the womb and the heart, a force of drawing in, pulling forth, stirring something ancient within me.

She spoke of dream-time, of the way the plants whisper through the veil of sleep. She taught me that to truly know her kin, one must step into the world of dreams.

When she is in bloom, I honour her presence more deeply, crafting a Mugwort pillow and taking a little tincture before sleep. It is on these nights that her voice is strongest, weaving visions, unravelling secrets, and guiding me through the twilight paths of dream and knowing. I have done this ever since, and every time she comes dancing.

Amisrel

Green girl gliding
Opening doors
Dream dancer
Bliss giver
Opener of ways
Aphrodite and Selene's wild child
I see you everywhere
Waving your silver hands
Teaching me to trust and not to doubt
Opening my mind
So that I can see…
The shadows of the Green.

A D O L - R W N G - F A

THE CHURCHYARD YEW

Yew

Culpeper on Yew

It grows to be an irregular tree, spreading widely into branches. The leaves are long, narrow, and placed with a beautiful regularity. The flowers are yellowish, and the berries are surrounded with a sweet juicy matter.

Place

We have it growing in woods, and in the gardens, but its usual ancient residence is the church-yard: conjectures upon the antiquity and origin of which plantatin, has brought forth much pedantic nonsense.

Gray observes in his poem the Grave

"Well do I know thee by thy trusty Yew,
"Shading for years thy gloomy church-yard view;
"Cheerless, unsocial plant, that loves to dwell
"Where scatter'd bones man's dissolution tell."

Government and virtues

This is a tree of Saturn. The leaves are said to be poisonous; but the wood, if it grew with more regularity would be very valuable. This tree, though it has no place among the physical plants, yet does it not deserve (at least in our climate) so bad a character as the ancients give it, viz. a most poisonous vegetable, the berries of which threaten present death to man and beast that eat them; many in this country having eaten them and survived. However that be, it has very powerful poisonous qualities, that rise by distillation. In this form it is the most active vegetable poison known in the whole world, for in a very small dose it instantly induces death without any previous disorder; and its deleterious power seems to act entirely upon the nervous system, and without exciting the least inflammation in the part to which it more immediately enters. It totally differs from opium and all other sleepy poisons, for it does not bring on the lethargic symptoms, but more effectually penetrates and destroys the vital functions, without immediately affecting the animal. These observations would not have been made, or the article inserted here, but to caution against any rash application of it, for though it is sometimes given useful in obstructions of the liver and bilious complaints, those experiments seem too few to recommend it to be used without the greatest caution. The deleterious qualities of laurel-water are more than equalled by this.

Charubel's commentary on the Yew

The pedigree of this tree and that of its numerous allies is a parallel with the Fir tree, to which it bears a rather striking resemblance; but which is, after all, of a different order.

The Yew is an order of plant life that partakes of both the Fern and the Fir. It may be said to form a connecting link between these two. In the order of cosmic development the Yew stands anterior to the Fir or the Pine. The Yew adapts itself to any country, and that without but very few changes in its structural appearance.

The Yew grows to a large tree in China. In Japan its leaves resemble the foliage of the Maiden-hair Fern; in the meantime it is with our grand old English Yew that I am now concerned. This tree grew in Britain ever since it was an island. It may be truly said to be indigenous to this island, and grew here when no other save the Fern tree abounded.

Thus the Yew was the first of flowering and fruit bearing plants then on this island. It thus stood forth as an indexfinger pointing to a new state of development, whilst its leaves point, to some extent, to a dead past, its fruit points towards a better and more hopeful future. Whilst the leaves of this tree are poisonous, the fruit is luscious, and are eaten by birds and children. This tree absorbs and dispenses. It absorbs the death principles of its surroundings, and gives out the life principle. Thus you may perceive, in what I say of this tree, that its being the connecting link between the Fern and the Fir, it is rational to suppose the one nature should absorb the evil, and the other should give out the good. The Ancients, in the far past, looked on this tree as being the Symbol of the planet Saturn and the Sun. Saturn stands for all things mortal, or the termination of the earthy. The Sun, as the beginning of a life that shall not be subject to decay and death. Thus the English Yew as it stands at this day in our old graveyards; more especially the old churchyards of Wales, where it abounds to a greater extent than in England; is a very proper Symbol for the mortal and the immortal; death and life; it has been planted by pious hands in our rural village graveyards, as a fit and proper symbol of it and immortality which came to light by the Gospel; and has been made use of in the past ages as the emblem of the Messiah, who took on Himself that nature which had become the subject of death, and in the meantime, by those higher powers of life which He possessed, developed the immortal. Thus out of death came life, as it was out of darkness that light came. There is a very pleasing disparity between the beautiful pink berries of the Yew tree and its sombre evergreen and poisonous leaves. There is a much more pleasing disparity between the mortal and the immortal in man. The mortal descends, but the immortal ascends. No one can tell the age of some Yews which I have seen in some of those little out of the way churchyards among the mountains of Wales. I counted seven in a small churchyard among the hills in Denbighshire. But these grand old trees abound and occupy large spaces in most country churchyards; they give a very picturesque aspect to rural villages, which I consider calculated to produce a very pleasing effect on the soul of the thoughtful.

The psychic virtue of the Yew Tree

On the psychic plane, this tree appears in a different costume. Its dark-green foliage is transformed into golden, mingled with azure.

From every branch, I see a small hair-like stream descending of what looks like Crystalline Nectar. I see an innumerable host of fairy-like beings about this tree, resembling a species of diminutive humanity. Each of these tiny beings is drinking at these crystal currents.

These beings appear to be primarily allied to the Yew tree. They are not only feeders on this tree themselves, but they can be made the distributors of its virtues to those whose soul may have an affinity to the sphere of the Yew. I do feel grateful to heaven for so glorious a revelation; and although but few of my readers will be sufficiently interested in this revelation to become the recipients of these mystic virtues, for I, for one, shall be benefited; seeing I make known to all what I receive, if others are nor benefited it will nor be my fault. This tree is not especially for any one form of the disease or such as are recognised as a disease. It has more to do with the soul of the individual.

Its virtues are expressly to build up the soul, which is the spiritual body. You may have read those words uttered by King David in one of his Psalms: "O spare me that I may recover strength before I go hence and be no more". It is evident that the Psalmist needed his soul strengthened. He must have had, for the time, a glimpse of another and interior body, which needed some little repairs before pulling down the old house. There was an epoch in the far past when man lived more on the psychic than on the so called intellectual plane; this is more than what the present humanity is capable of realising.

Our present conceptions of beauty are not in unison with those possessed by man during one of those buried eons of the past. Nature closes each door after the birth of her offspring. Thus when one race has completed its round, fulfilled its mission, the door of that degree attained to by that race is closed behind it. The succeeding humanity cannot form any idea as to what may be the conceptions of its predecessor, but the predecessor may form correct notions of its successor. In the meantime, as there are always exceptions to every rule, or in other words, there ever have been those who have tried, whilst members of the succeeding race, the life of its predecessor, and have been able to realise what may have been the leading ideas of that race. But, when these exceptional characters seek to make these same ideas known to their contemporaries, they are sure to be misunderstood, and what they say or write, for the time, will not be appreciated.

This tree was known to the Psychic race, who were able to imbibe from its branches, as it appeared to them in that life and on that plane of existence, a support which the humanity of this heady race have no conceptions of. Clairvoyance approaches that condition; at the same time, neither Clairvoyance, Clairaudience, nor Psychometry are to be considered identical with that state.

It is vain consulting an ordinary disembodied spirit as to the nature of this Psychic race, much more useless to consult modern scientists. There is a phase of untutored and unspoiled childhood, which bears a more striking resemblance to psychic man than any other outward embodiment that I am acquainted with. Hence the applicability of those words of Jesus: "Except ye become as a little child, ye cannot see the kingdom of heaven". That child to whom the Master alluded was not the spoiled, sharp, or precocious child of this nineteenth century, which I design the heady race, being the antithesis of the soul race.

What I write is but a fragment of the experience of that everyday life I am living on the soul plane. The psychic side of nature with her boundless resources are as familiar to me as the hills and valleys of my native land. I come in contact with more there than can be found here; hence the Yew appears more marvellous to me than it does to you. I am not at all surprised that the good old men of the past should have chosen this tree as Monarch of the graveyard and companion of the dead!

I hope I may never see the day when this heady race will have attained that degree of turpitude as to cut down this Grand Old Relic of a long lost past; and Survivor of the Cosmic wreck. The noble Oak has been partially destroyed; and as a result the present race is weakened on the outer plane. Should any one presumptuously in my presence take up the axe to fell the Yew I will cry out, not sing out, "Goodman spare that tree, touch not a single bough". In it a past eternity unites the present now.

Who among my readers are capable of being benefited by the psychic nature of the Yew? Those who are highly sympathetic; those who are impressionable; those whose minds are not absorbed in the things of the senses, those who are fond of solitude; those who delight in the contemplation of nature where it is most natural; not the most accomplished; not the most highly educated; nor yet the most extraordinary intellect. As a rule, it may be calculated that the more ordinary samples of humanity are suitable for the reception of those influences and virtues that this beautiful tree possesses.

It has been already stated that the Yew tree is a soul strengthener; but this phrase is scarcely sufficiently comprehensive; I will further say, it includes lowness of spirits, or a sense of great depression, and that when there is nothing in the circumstances of the individual to constitute a real cause for such a state. All such symptoms indicate a weak or infirm soul; and when manifested through the brain, or the outer consciousness, is insanity. There is no radical cure for this kind of disorder in the Therapeutics of Medical Science. Nor are there but few of the Profession so bold as to pretend that drugs may cure such. Instead of medicine, they generally advise a change of scenery, cheerful company, or a sea voyage. In the meantime, there must be a remedy, but that remedy must be of such a nature as to be capable of reaching the afflicted part, or primary seat of such an affliction. I have, in the Yew, discovered a remedy that will absorb that morbific effluvia, which, like the horrid nightmare, clings to the helpless soul—the spiritual body—and at the same time impart to those psychic wounds a healing balm. Connected with the cure are rules and observances to be complied with, as well as an Invocation to be uttered, the whole should be strictly and religiously observed. The best time to apply to the Yew for help is the seventh hour past noon. The patient or his helper should devote the greater part of the hour to these meditations, either in reading what I have written respecting it or thinking on the tree itself.

To get the right expression of this word, fancy it being spelt thus: Adol-roong-va. Go over it seven times. At an age like the present, when the epidemic of suicides is on the increase, it becomes you to make use of this soul remedy.

Charubel's Name—ADOL RWNG FA
Personal Name—ION

Charubel's Psychic sigil

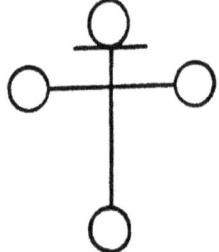

Personal Sigil

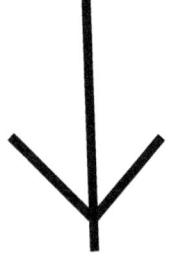

Saturn Kamea sigil

Alchemical practice

All parts of the Yew are poisonous so you must take great care when handling any part of it. Do not diet this plant. Make your tincture from the body of the Arils. I used the Arils, particularly with this seed's potential. The idea is that the Yew is showing you potential in the future and in your soul rather than accepting what is. I did my alchemical extraction when the Moon was in Aquarius, and there was an excellent aspect to Saturn. This has not been difficult in the last few years as currently Saturn has had a strong dignity.

Yew mythology

There are so many myths surrounding the Yew that I would recommend much further study. The idea that Yggdrasil was a Yew rather than Ash speaks to me after working with this tree. When the Yew's branches touch the floor another tree is born–thus it is truly immortal. There are also the myths of the Yew being the original Tree of Life with the beautiful story of the three Yew arils placed into Adam's mouth at his death. These grew into the White, Golden, and Red trees. The White is the Staff of Moses, the Green is the Burning Bush, and the Red is the father of all Yews today. The stories around the Gods born of the trees are outlined in a wonderful book called *The God Tree* by Janis Fry. This is quite a rare book now, but I highly recommend it.

Medical use of the Yew

The Yew is the basis for the chemotherapy drug Tamoxifen or Taxol.

Taxol targets microtubules, which are dynamic structures made of tubulin proteins that play a critical role in cell division. Normally, microtubules constantly assemble and disassemble, creating a dynamic structure essential for mitosis (cell division). During mitosis, microtubules form the mitotic spindle, which separates duplicated chromosomes into two daughter cells.

Taxol disrupts this process by stabilizing microtubules and preventing their disassembly. This "freezing" of microtubules halts the dynamic changes required for the spindle apparatus to function properly. As a result, cancer cells are unable to complete mitosis, leading to a mitotic arrest. This triggers a series of stress responses within the cell, often culminating in apoptosis (programmed cell death). Breast and ovarian cancers, which often feature high rates of cell division, are particularly susceptible to Taxol's effects.

In this way, the Yew truly embodies its mythological reputation as a tree of both life and death. It harbours poison yet gives life-saving medicine. It stands as a timeless witness to the cycles of nature and humanity.

Magical use of the Yew

The Yew is, without a doubt, one of the most magical of trees, a guardian of mysteries and a keeper of deep, old wisdom. It holds a place of utmost importance in my coven, not just as a powerful ally but as a living presence woven into our practice. This is the tree from which the Runes were drawn, steeped in the magic of divination, fate, and the weaving of the unseen. It is also sacred to Hekate, the queen of witches, the torchbearer at the crossroads, and the guide through shadowed realms.

Magically, the Yew is a tree of binding and holding, making it invaluable for spells that require containment, protection, or sealing something firmly in place. This comes from its deep connection to Saturn, the planet of structure, limitation, and the inexorable passage of time. But its Saturnine nature goes beyond that—it is also a tree of death and transformation, standing as a bridge between worlds.

Yews are ancient, and their presence in graveyards is no accident. They do not just mark places of rest; they whisper of what lies beyond. Their slow, steady growth, their ability to regenerate from within their own hollows, and their sheer longevity make them a powerful symbol of death and rebirth, endings and new beginnings. This makes them potent allies in work with the underworld, ancestral magic, and rites of passage.

But, as with all such beings, the Yew demands respect. It is not a tree to be approached lightly. It holds poison in its body, a quiet but firm warning that its gifts are not to be taken thoughtlessly. This is a tree of depth, of patience, of things that move beneath the surface, unseen but ever-present. To work with Yew is to step into a relationship with time itself, with the spaces between life and death, with the silent knowledge that lingers long after all else has faded.

Personal observations

Astrologically, I feel that Yew is Saturn in Aquarius. It teaches about boundaries but not as obstacles; instead, it shows you ways to deal with limitations and how to work with them, that is, around them rather than just accepting them as they appear.

Yew is a slow tree, it is almost immortal, and it took an extraordinarily long time to get any form of relationship with it. But when I began working with it, the results were terrific! I learnt about the cyclic nature and movement from death to life and back again. The spirit asked me this: "You all worry about life after death; why does no one ask about life before birth".

After my mother passed, I found myself drawn to the Yew circle in Llanfeugan, Brecon. Standing among those ancient trees, I felt their presence wrap around me, steady and knowing. It was there, in that quiet communion, that Yew revealed itself to me. A crow-headed figure cloaked in black, a great staff in hand, wreathed in the scent of burnt charcoal and damp earth. It was the smell of late autumn, that fleeting moment when October gives way to November, the aroma of decay, and the whisper of something waiting beyond the disintegration. And in that space, the name I received was Ion.

Ion did not speak of death as an end, but as movement. Life does not simply stop; it shifts, it transforms. What we call death is not destruction, but transition, energy changing shape, carrying experience from one form to another. Yew teaches us to see through three sets of eyes at once: the child, the parent, and the aged. Each holds a different thread of understanding, yet all are part of the same weave. There is no finality, no great abyss to fear, just the passage through one door into another way of being. The last breath here is the first breath there, wherever there may be. No fear, no punishment, no hell, only movement, ever onward.

Ion showed me two truths that altered both my practice and my way of seeing the world. The first was a lesson in time itself. We try to pin it down and measure it in smaller increments, but the more we dissect it, the more it slips through our fingers. Yew challenges our rigid ideas of past, present, and future. It reminds us that just living is enough. You do not need to break something apart to understand it.

The second truth was one of balance. Growth without limits is not life, but a sickness—cancerous, consuming. The natural order is not a straight line of endless expansion, but a cycle: growth, decay, renewal. Each feeds the next, each is essential. Without death, there is no space for new beginnings, no nourishment for what comes after. The fertile ground of tomorrow is built upon what has been surrendered today. To resist this truth, to cling desperately to permanence, is to deny the very nature of existence itself. Life is not static, it is a dance, a rhythm, a constant unfolding of endings and beginnings, creation and dissolution, forever in motion.

A personal spirit appearance

Ion came to me as a crow-headed figure, cloaked in black, a great staff in hand. When I sat with the Yew, Ion sat with me. Not speaking, not instructing, just being. A presence as old as stone, as steady as the turning of the seasons. He did not offer words, nor did he need to. The lesson was in the silence, in the unwavering stillness, in the way the world continued to breathe around us. He was there, patient, constant, watching.

There was no rush, no grand revelation, only the deep, quiet knowing that comes from simply existing beside something ancient. Yew does not demand. It does not explain. It waits. And in that waiting, in that shared breath of time stretching out and folding in, something settled within me. A truth, unspoken but understood; sometimes the greatest wisdom is found in silence.

The energy from the tree was immense, a being of immeasurable wisdom and knowledge, but one for whom you must have the most profound respect.

ION

Being of time
Sitting in the land of the dead
Counting the years as minutes by your clock
Scarred and red
The crows find homes within you
And are drawn upon your face
Toads at your base and dragons in your depths
You speak to the soul of all things
Dark are you, wet and deep and slow, so slow
Looking out across the land where Romans ploughed Yesterday
for you, ancient history for us
We are fleeting in your eye
Buzzing across your sentience
Gone before we know it
While you stand, sentinel to time.

MUR-ROO

THE POPPY

Poppy

Culpeper on Poppy

Description

The stalk of this Poppy is thick and naked, round, and fleshy. The leaves are but few, and grow irregularly; they are stripped into many deep divided segments, and of a pale green colour. the flower is large and single, growing at the top of the stalk; the usual colour of it is a bright scarlet; but sometimes it is yellow or white. In the middle is a tuft of yellow threads. Cultivation has produced many varieties of this plant.

Place

They are found wild in great abundance in Asia, but in England they are only found in gardens.

Time

It flowers in June.

Government and Virtues

The acrid and caustic quality of this Poppy declare it to be of Saturn's reign, but still it should not be totally overlooked, as it is of good service to move warts. It is the juice of the plant expressed, some use that to make way for the instruments of surgery; and the whole plant bruised has been applied by others to move the headache, but care must be taken not to let it come too near the eyes, as it will cause inflammation.

Poppy mythology

In ancient Greek mythology, the *Hypnos*, *Nyx* and *Thanatos* characters all had the Poppy as their sacred symbol, as did the Greek goddess *Demeter* and the Roman goddess *Ceres*. The Poppy was seen as giving lifeblood to the soil, nourishing the grains, and life, fertility, and death. I see shades of the sacrifice of John Barleycorn to fertilise the land here, where you see the red Poppy heads waving amongst the wheat fields.

Charubel on Poppy

Crimson corn Poppy (Papaver rhoeas). This has been fitly called a Brilliant Weed. It frequents waste places and is more abundant in the Southern Counties than in the North.

This BEAUTIFUL plant is a lover of cornfields, which you can easily see at some distance as the deep crimson bloom renders it so conspicuous, and even attractive. It appears to vie with those prouder and much petted beauties of the flower garden.

Indeed as an annual there is not one that can surpass it in richness of colour. The Poppy as a class possesses great tenacity to life; the seed will remain dormant in the ground for years.

This is the case when a field that has been long under cultivation is laid down to grass, where the Poppy has abounded and flourished for years; once the field becomes grass the Poppy is seen no longer; at the same time, after a long period of years, when the same field is again under cultivation, the Poppy will again show itself.

This has been noticed in deep railway cuttings where the Crimson Poppy has shown itself the first year. These seeds must have slumbered for ages.

I am quite aware that some modern time writers will account for such from other sources than those I have mentioned. Yet I do not see any reason why we should doubt the possibility of a seed, shut out from the light and air, being capable of retaining its vitality for centuries. But to ensure this, the seed must while in its vigour, be in fact hermetically sealed. There are about 180 species of the Poppy tribe known, two-thirds of which belong to Europe, the remainder are scattered over the globe. I now come to deal with this beautiful annual psychically and psychomedically. The question, which arises here, as elsewhere: For what purpose has this plant been projected on the Physical Plane. For every plant, great and small, has its mission; that mission has been of a far higher order than to please the eye of thousands of superficially minded pleasure seekers, who oft with cruel and ruthless hands will devastate a whole neighbourhood of its lovely floral companions, and that for no other purpose than to hold them, to droop and die, in the hand for a few hours. So much loveliness has not been born simply for you to gaze on. The bloom of every plant and tree is the bridal dress of that plant. The insect tribes in general, and the bee in particular, are fascinated and attracted by those gay colours. It is in fact an invitation to all to come to the floral marriage. When the little cups are filled with the ambrosial nectar the pollen it is also ready to be taken from the otherwise barren bloom to fructify one, when the bees and insects are liable to intermix them, owing to the pollen sticking to the insects by the aid of the honey, which must adhere to them. Thus nature pays her little workers for services, which they unconsciously render. Seeing such wonders are discoverable on the physical plane, in these strange adaptations and wonderful design; what must be the condition of such plants on the higher planes of floral life? Have we not here proofs of higher and grander designs? Yes, verily, to my knowledge we have. What I tell you in this paper is no guesswork it is knowledge. I will here give you the result of this knowledge respecting this little plant, the Crimson Cornfield Poppy. It is a plant on the soul plane; it is a plant in bloom; it appears of the same colour on the soul plane as on the physical. It lives on the soul plane yes, it lives! But that life is not conditioned as it is now on the earth plane. Its roots do not feed by suction or of the damp, cold earth. It lives by imbibing other essences. It is a living thing, and more than that, it is a semi-intelligent thing. Whilst the plant life is incarcerated in an organised body on earth it often manifests a kind of instinct not far removed from that animal life which may subsequently feed on the plant life. But when it has left its tiny tabernacle on the earth plane, it forms for itself a superior and a more beautiful dwelling, a form which the nipping frosts of winter may not injure, or rude hand destroy. It henceforth lives for the health and happiness of higher intelligences, whom it will serve with its odour as well as its life-sustaining aura.

These plants are all living, semi-intelligent entities, and that man who has advanced to their soul plane, may by sympathy, inhale from those ambrosial fonts health, life, and happiness. It is thus, and in this light I see the present plant bedecked in its gorgeous bridal bloom. Its petals will not fade! It is no longer chained to one poor spot of earth, but freely and majestically floats upon the ether-wave, and may thus become the companion of some solitary soul, who may have looked in vain for sympathy from his fellows.

In these papers I point out the simple way by which the partially developed soul may attract to itself whilst in the body, what may help under sorrow and suffering of various kinds. The animal kingdom are incapable of such virtues from their psychic state.

The complaints for which the Crimson Poppy is adapted. It constitutes a remedy for:

i. A deep dull pain in the forehead; more especially at the centre of the forehead with a great heaviness about the eyes and eyelids.
ii. An intolerable want to sleep, but after sleep not refreshed.
iii. Averse to all intellectual labour, living in a kind of stupor state, not unlike the effects from having imbibed a narcotic.

The word for invocation is MUR-ROO:

The word by which you may use to call, command, or invoke the virtue of this beautiful plant is MUR-ROO The word should be repeated nine times.

Charubel's Name:
MUR-ROO
Charubel's Sigil

Personal Name:
PA RE
Personal Sigil

Saturn Kamea Sigil

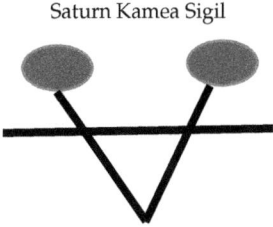

Modern research

The Poppy plant (Papaver somniferum) has long been a cornerstone in pharmacology, primarily due to its production of opium, a substance rich in alkaloids such as morphine, codeine, and papaverine. These compounds have been instrumental in medicine for their potent analgesic and antitussive properties.

Morphine, derived from the Opium Poppy, remains unparalleled in its efficacy for alleviating severe pain, such as that experienced during myocardial infarction. Its ability to bind to opioid receptors in the central nervous system makes it a critical component in pain management protocols.

Papaverine, another significant alkaloid found in the Poppy, is utilised for its antispasmodic effects. It is commonly employed in treating visceral spasms and vasospasms, particularly those affecting the intestines, heart, or brain. Additionally, papaverine has applications in managing erectile dysfunction and acute mesenteric ischemia.

Codeine, also extracted from the Opium Poppy, serves as an effective antitussive agent. It is frequently included in cough syrups and cold medications to suppress persistent coughing, owing to its ability to decrease the activity of the cough reflex.

While the pharmacological benefits of Poppy-derived compounds are well-established, it is crucial to acknowledge the risks associated with their use. The potential for dependence and abuse necessitates careful medical supervision.

Dieting the plant

Please remember that this is a plant that provides opiates.

With that in mind you can make a very dilute tea of the Poppy seeds and also use the Poppy seeds on bread or muffins to ingest that way.

NB: Take care with the tea for it produces euphoric results and can lead to addiction.

Personal experience

One of the things I absolutely love about working with the Poppy is the way our relationship has shaped the plant itself. I planted her when we first moved into this house, nearly 30 years ago, and for the longest time, she did very little. A single, stunning bloom now and then, but never more than one, as if she were testing the waters but not quite ready to commit.

Then I started working with her spirit and she *exploded* into bloom.

To me, she is pure Saturn, but not just any Saturn; she carries the energy of Saturn in Scorpio. There is something both commanding and magnetic about her presence. She is prickly but loving, drawing you in even as she warns you to handle her with care. She *wants* to be seen, to be touched, to be known, and yet, there is an edge to her—a sharpness woven through her beauty. She is both acerbic and sensuous, both a guardian and an invitation. A paradox in silk and thorn, standing tall, radiant, and entirely on her own terms.

Meditation

When I first approached her, she appeared as a priestess robed in red, veiled in deep purple. The air around her was thick with something unspoken, something whispered rather than declared. She did not speak of sleep as a gentle descent into rest, but as a slow, languid surrender—a slipping into dreaming sequences of sex and wetness, of secrets murmured behind heavy-lidded eyes.

Her hair was white, stark against the endless black of her eyes. When she spoke, her voice carried the weight of necessity. She told me that to survive, in magic and in life, one must see both potential and labour—desire alone is never enough. She spoke of persistence, of the need to carve ground with both will and effort, of the way nothing is ever truly given, only earned.

She turned my gaze to the realm of dreams, the unseen world of ideas, the place where thought shapes reality before it ever takes form. She whispered that the unconscious is not just a place of wandering but a kingdom of architects, where the foundations of the waking world are laid. It is in dreams that the bones of creation are set, that the unseen scaffolds of our lives are built, waiting to be drawn into being.

She is not a gentle guide. She demands. At times, she lectures, her tone sharp with the impatience of a teacher unwilling to indulge laziness. But beneath the sternness, there is kindness, a steady presence reminding me that persistence is the heart of all great work. Again and again, she returned to this, keep going, keep pushing, keep weaving.

She reclined as she spoke, stretched across a low bed, at ease in her power. And I, cross-legged on the floor, sat like a child at her feet, drinking in her words, waiting for the lessons that would shape me.

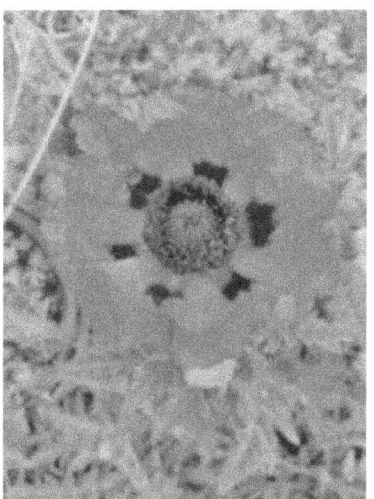

From the first year of working to my fully blossomed Poppy jungle.

Alchemical praxis

I tinctured Poppy when the Moon was in Scorpio with an excellent aspect to Saturn. I used both flower and leaf for the tincture to gain both elements: the astringency of Saturn, and the sensuousness of Scorpio. The result was a very odd coloured tincture, as the pollen for this plant is purple. I used the old-fashioned tincture method for the Poppy as she was delicate, and I felt she needed a longer tincture time than that of the planetary hour.

Pa Re

Daughter of Hypnos
Showing the way to the land of sleep
Sensual, sexual, wet and dripping
White sap oozing
Black seeds bringing dreams into the world
Red of Barleycorn's blood, given for the brown bowl Soldier's sister, giving her all on the battlefields
Joyous in the dying and the dead
Rebirth and Reawakening the routes of our journey

L U ‑ V A R ‑ M E L

MONKSHOOD

Monkshood

Culpeper on Monkshood

Description

The plant is a hardy perennial, with a fleshy, spindle-shaped root, pale coloured when young, but subsequently acquiring a dark brown skin. The stem is about three feet high, with dark green, glossy leaves, deeply divided in palmate manner and flowers in erect clusters of a dark blue colour. The shape of the flower is specially designed to attract and utilize bee visitors, especially the humble bee. The sepals are purple–purple being especially attractive to bees–and are fancifully shaped, one of them being in the form of a hood. The petals are only represented by the two very curious nectars within the hood, somewhat in the form of a hammer; the stamens are numerous and lie depressed in a bunch at the mouth of the flower. They are pendulous at first, but rise in succession and place their anthers forward in such a way that a bee visiting the flower for nectar is dusted with the pollen, which he then carries to the next flower he visits and thereby fertilizes the undeveloped fruits, which are in a tuft in the centre of the stamens, each carpel containing a single seed.

In the Anglo-Saxon vocabularies it is called thung, which seems to have been a general name for any very poisonous plant. It was then called Aconite (the English form of its Greek and Latin name), later Wolf's Bane, the direct translation of the Greek Lycotonum, derived from the idea that arrows tipped with the juice, or baits anointed with it, would kill wolves–the species mentioned by Dioscorides seems to have been Aconitum lycotonum. In the Middle Ages it became Monkshood and Helmetflower, from the curious shape of the upper sepal overtopping the rest of the flower. This was the ordinary name in Shakespeare's days.

Monkshood mythology

All aconite species are associated with Magic and are sacred to Hekate and Medea. According to Ovid, a vengeful Athena had beaten the young and talented *Arachne*, daughter of *Idmon*, and the girl then hanged herself on a tree where she was magically transformed into a spider. The plant therefore can allow one the ability to shape-shift. One of its names is *wolfsbane*, indicating its protective function used against wolves. Hunters would spike meat with wolfsbane seeds, and which would poison the wolves after they ate the meat. It is therefore a potent poison and is included in many magical flying ointments. These demonstrate its potentiality by aiding practitioners to literally "fly", by means of altering their magical perception.

Charubel on Monkshood

The Monkshood is the most poisonous of the Crowfoot family. The sepals and petals of its flower are purple-coloured. There are five sepals, and one of these is very large and resembles a kind of helmet, which overshadows the other part of the flower; only two of the petals are fully developed. These are two fleshy bodies mounted on long stalks, projecting into the helmet. Both leaves and roots of this plant are very poisonous, the roots especially so. It flowers in July; and thrives best in damp places.

This plant may be found in most flower gardens, and not infrequently its roots are in proximity to those vegetables, which are used as edibles. Thus you may have in your gardens one of the ninety-four most virulent of vegetable poisons over which there may be but little care, or caution exercised.

There is one peculiar characteristic connected with this plant; heat destroys or extracts the poison of the Monkshood branches in a very short time. If the branches be cut and exposed to the hot sun for but a few days they become harmless.

To administer this plant as a medicine for any known complaint is very unsafe, unless it is made along Homeopathic lines, or under the surveillance of a professional practitioner. Not so is this the case on the soul plane. Here this plant may safely be applied without any danger of evil consequences.

It is this safety, and security, in the Psychology of Botany, which renders it of so much service, and value, to all who are interested in its application.

Colds and chills are of frequent occurrence in a climate like our own, where we are subject to sudden changes from heat to cold in summer, and from dry to damp at all times and seasons. How often is it the case, that after free perspiration you sit in some cool place, and a chill is the result, yes, a chill, which in many instances proves fatal. Would you consider a safe remedy at hand, of any value? I give you this remedy freely at that critical moment.

When you feel a chill from any cause whatever, and under any circumstances, think of the Monkshood, picture it before your mind's eye, and whilst doing so, repeat the following invocationary word: LU-VAR-MEL, six times, most deliberately and reverentially, then allow the subject to rest for two hours, when you repeat the same a second time. It is rarely necessary you should repeat a third time. The usual symptoms subside, and a warm glow succeeds the chill; afterwards, avoid undue exposure.

Modern research into Monkshood

Monkshood has always been a bit of a rebellious character, beautiful, powerful, and completely unwilling to play nice with modern medicine. Despite having a solid historical résumé in traditional Chinese and Ayurvedic healing, where it was used for pain relief, reducing inflammation, and even matters of the heart (literally, as a cardiotonic), it remains stubbornly dangerous. Of course, those old healers knew better than to use it carelessly; preparing Monkshood properly was an art in itself, because getting it wrong meant a swift and unpleasant end.

In Western herbal traditions, Monkshood was once a well-respected painkiller, easing everything from nerve pain and arthritis to gout and sciatica. It was even used to manage fevers and inflammation, until of course its lethal tendencies became a bit too obvious, and modern medicine decided it was more trouble than it was worth.

And here is where it gets interesting, because despite plenty of evidence that Monkshood does have useful applications, it refuses to cooperate. It has a very narrow therapeutic window, which is science-speak for "the difference between healing and horrible death is uncomfortably small". Modern pharmacology has tried to tame it, but Monkshood, true to form, remains unyielding. It is as if the plant itself is saying, "I could help you, but honestly, I just do not feel like it".

Personal experience

I have always found Monkshood difficult to know. She does not give herself freely, nor does she care to be coaxed. It took me years to even begin to breach her walls, and even now, I am not entirely sure she tolerates me so much as she has resigned herself to my persistence.

She resisted tincturing, outright refused to yield to the process. Perhaps this year, as she grows, she will allow me to make an essence instead. But I have learned not to push. She made it clear that she was not interested in working through tinctures, though she did confirm her uses—helpful in fevers that make one sweat, calming to nervousness. Yet the way she spoke of this so-called calm made my skin prickle. It was not the soft hush of eased anxieties, but something far darker, a stillness that felt more like a final silence than a gentle soothing.

When she did appear in meditation, she came as an older woman, dressed in black, a woven basket on her arm. She looked every bit like the ancient Greek women you still see gathering herbs in the hills—practical, weathered, knowing. But there was a grin, sharp and wicked, the kind that tells you she enjoys keeping her secrets. She carries something dark, something untamed, something entirely her own. She is not a plant that seeks out relationships with humans, or perhaps, she just found me particularly irritating.

She did not speak, until I moved her. I had planted her in my herb garden at first, but she withered there, sulking at the sun and the well-ordered neatness of it all. It was only when I shifted her to the dark, damp part of the lower garden that she finally broke her silence. She liked it there, in the mud and the wet, half-lost among the shadows. And there, she spoke.

She whispered of the soil, of what we all become in the end. That no matter how we fight it, no matter what spells we weave or prayers we offer, we will all return to the earth, to the damp, black loam, to the great and endless cycle. It was not a threat, nor was it a comfort. Simply a truth, laid bare.

For me, she is Venus in Capricorn. An old understanding, a knowing beyond time. She is poison and magic, limits and thresholds, the silent watcher at the edge of the veil. She does not offer herself freely, but if you truly listen, she will teach you what it means to embrace the witch soul.

Charubel Sigil

Charubel Name　　　　　　　　Personal Name
LU VAR MEL　　　　　　　　　MEHAL

Kamea Sigil from the Venus Kamea

RA‑MA‑IL

ROSEMARY

Rosemary

Culpeper on Rosemary

Time

It flowers in April and May with us, sometimes again in August.

Government and virtues

The Sun claims privilege in it, and it is under the celestial Ram. It is an herb of as great use with us in these days as any whatsoever, not only for physical but civil purposes. The physical use of it (being my present task) is very much used both for inward and outward diseases, for by the warming and comforting heat thereof it helps all cold diseases, both of the head, stomach, liver, and belly. The decoction thereof in wine helps the cold distillations of rheum into the eyes, and all other cold diseases of the head and brain, as the giddiness or swimming therein, drowsiness or dullness of the mind and senses like a stupid-ness, the dumb palsy, or loss of speech, the lethargy, and fallen-sickness, to be both drank, and the temples bathed therewith. It helps the pains in the gums and teeth, by rheum falling into them, not by putrefaction, causing an evil smell from them, or a stinking breath. It helps a weak memory, and quickens the senses. It is very comfortable to the stomach in all the cold grief thereof, helps both retention of meat, and digestion, the decoction or powder being taken in wine. It is a remedy for the windiness in the stomach, bowels, and spleen, and expels it powerfully. It helps those that are liver-grown, by opening the obstructions thereof. It helps dim eyes, and procures a clear sight, the flowers thereof being taken all the while it is flowering every morning fasting, with bread and salt. Both Dioscorides and Galen say, That if a decoction be made thereof with water, and they that have the yellow jaundice exercise their bodies directly after the *taking* thereof, it will certainly cure them. The flowers and conserve made of them, are singularly good to comfort the heart, and to expel the contagion of the pestilence; to burn the herb in houses and chambers corrects the air in them. Both the flowers and leaves are very profitable for women that are troubled with the whites, if they be daily taken. The dried leaves shred small, and taken in a pipe, as tobacco is taken, helps those that have any cough, phthisic, or consumption, by warming and drying the thin distillations which cause those diseases. The leaves are very much used in bathing; and made into ointments or oil, are singularly good to help cold benumbed joints, sinews, or members. The chymical oil drawn from the leaves and flowers is a sovereign help for all the diseases aforesaid, to touch the temples and nostrils with two or three drops for all the diseases of the head and brain spoken of before; as also to take one drop, two, or three, as the case requires, for the inward grief: Yet must it be done with discretion, for it is very quick and piercing, and therefore but a little must be taken at a time. There is also another oil made by insolation in this manner: Take what quantity you will of the flowers, and put them into a strong glass close stopped, tie a fine linen cloth over the mouth, and turn the mouth down into another strong glass, which being set in the sun, an oil will distil down into the lower glass, to be preserved as precious for divers uses, both inward and outward, as a sovereign balm to heal the disease before-mentioned, to clear dim sights, and to take away spots, marks, and scars in the skin.

Charubel on Rosemary

No reference to Rosemary in the grimoire.

Modern research on Rosemary

Modern research into Rosemary (Rosmarinus officinalis) has uncovered a wealth of fascinating properties, confirming much of what traditional wisdom has long held to be true while also revealing new dimensions to this extraordinary herb.

Rosemary has shown remarkable neuroprotective effects, thanks to its potent antioxidant and anti-inflammatory compounds like carnosic acid and rosmarinic acid. These compounds help protect brain cells from oxidative stress and degeneration, making Rosemary a promising candidate in the study of neurodegenerative conditions such as Alzheimer's disease.

Beyond that, Rosemary's long-standing association with memory is not just folklore; modern science supports it. Both consuming and inhaling Rosemary have been linked to improved memory and cognitive function, reinforcing its role as a herb of remembrance in both the literal and symbolic sense.

Research also suggests that Rosemary has adaptogenic qualities, meaning it can help the body manage stress more effectively. It has been shown to lower cortisol levels, stabilise mood, and improve mental clarity. Its influence on neurotransmitter systems suggests it could play a role in reducing anxiety and stress-related conditions, offering a natural boost to resilience and well-being.

Some of the most exciting studies focus on Rosemary's potential anti-cancer properties. Certain compounds within the plant appear to slow the growth of cancer cells and even encourage apoptosis, the process of programmed cell death. These effects have been particularly noted in colon and prostate cancers, making Rosemary a subject of growing interest in complementary medicine.

One of the more unexpected yet thoroughly exciting discoveries is Rosemary's ability to promote hair growth. Studies comparing Rosemary oil to minoxidil (a well-known treatment for hair loss) found it to be just as effective in stimulating hair regrowth. Better yet, Rosemary oil was gentler on the scalp, reducing irritation and itching, making it an excellent natural alternative for those looking to support healthy hair.

Alchemical practice

I made a Hydrosol of Rosemary. I steam-distilled it, gaining a tiny amount of oil and a hydrosol that was just amazing. The smell of the oil was so strong that it almost took away my breath. The water was something that you could just lay in a bowl and allow the scent to permeate the house for days.

I prepared the hydrosol on a Sunday as close to midsummer as possible. I used a waxing Moon but did not use a Leo placement, as there was too much distance between the midsummer and the Moon in Leo.

Personal experience

Rosemary is beauty in every measure, a presence both strong and gentle. He greeted me with warmth, his energy steady and sure, and the perfume of his name, so rich, so sharp, sang in the air like an old song waiting to be remembered.

He works with the past, not just in the way of memory, but in understanding the deep workings of the world, the interwoven threads of time. He shines with the sun's energy, radiant and clear; in that light, he sees all things within the great circle of existence. This, I believe, is where his deep ties to remembrance and memory stem from.

It fascinates me that his mercurial cousin, Lavender, sharpens the mind, helping you recall facts and figures with precision. But Rosemary? Rosemary does something different. He takes you into the feeling of memory, into the scent of a summer long gone, the warmth of a hand no longer there, the echoes of laughter woven into the fabric of time. He does not just help you remember, he makes you relive.

If you can work with Rosemary, I urge you to do so. He is open, generous, and kind. A companion as much as a teacher, a guide through the landscapes of memory, and a guardian of the stories that shape us.

Meditational experience

He came to me like an old friend, one I had not seen in years but knew as if we had spoken only yesterday. That deep, familiar ease, the kind that settles in the bones. The connection was instant, warm, steady, and utterly natural, as if he had always been there, waiting.

He appeared as a farmer, dressed in earth's own colours, brown and beige, simple and unassuming. Yet there was a glow about him, something just beyond words, as though life itself ran through him in its purest form. He was well in a way that went deeper than flesh, as if rooted in something ancient and enduring.

His voice carried weight, strong and sure, a voice that did not demand but guided. And with that voice, he allowed me to lay certain things to rest, things that had lingered too long in the quiet corners of my mind.

He gave me the phrase: "I am the person I am because of these experiences, not despite them". And with that, the past shifted. He led me to the pain my mother had carried and laid it bare before me, but not as a wound or a weakness, simply as her truth. He showed me that she was not diminished by what she endured. She was herself, moving through life in the only way she knew how. And most of all, she loved us. That love, imperfect and raw, was still love.

That was his great gift to me. A new way of seeing. A loosening of old knots. My mother's way of living had shaped me in ways I had struggled to make peace with, but through him, I saw it clearly at last. Not as something to battle, not as something to resent, but as part of the weave of my own becoming.

Charubel Name	Personal Name
No name in the Grimoire	RA MA IL
Personal Sigil	Sun Kamea

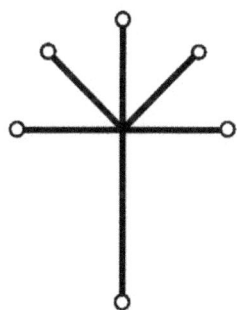 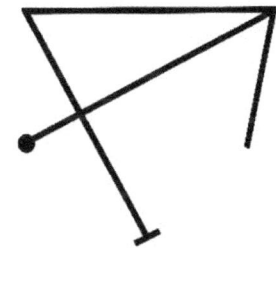

RA MA IL

    Smiling hand in the sunshine
    Leathery and warm
    The smell of safety and excited expectation
    Bringing memories long festering
    To the surface to be cleaned
    To once again hold glory and allow people to be seen

To give rest to the wicked and to be the poor man's guide
In remembering the truth, to expose the illusions in which we hide
I am me in all my glory, with my warts and all my joys Because of time I spent with you, with all your flaws thrown wide.
To learn to thank the passage, to learn to let it go
A gift beyond all reason
To love
To know
To grow

A P H - H I - M O O

MARSHMALLOW

Marshmallow

Culpeper on Marshmallow

Our common Marshmallows have divers soft hairy white stalks, rising to be three or four feet high, spreading forth many branches, the leaves whereof are soft and hairy, somewhat less than the other Mallow leaves, but longer pointed, cut (for the most part) into some few divisions, but deep. The flowers are many, but smaller also than the other Mallows, and white, or tending to a bluish colour. After which come such long, round cases and seeds, as in the other Mallows. The roots are many and long, shooting from one head, of the bigness of a thumb or finger, very pliant, tough, and being like liquorice, of a whitish yellow colour on the outside, and more whitish within, full of a slimy juice, which being laid in water, will thicken, as if it were a jelly.

Place

The common mallows grow in every county of this land. The common marsh-mallows in most of the salt marshes, from Woolwich down to the sea, both on the Kentish and Essex shores, and in divers other places of this land.

Time

> They flower all the Summer months, even until the Winter do pull them down.

Government and virtues

> Venus owns them both. The leaves of either of the sorts, both specified, and the roots also boiled in wine or water, or in broth with Parsley or Fennel roots, do help to open the body, and are very convenient in hot agues, or other distempers of the body, to apply the leaves so boiled warm to the belly. It not only voids hot, choleric, and other offensive humours, but eases the pains and torments of the belly coming thereby; and are therefore used in all clysters conducing to those purposes. The same used by nurses procures them store of milk. The decoction of the seed of any of the common Mallows made in milk or wine, doth marvellously help excoriations, the phthisic pleurisy, and other diseases of the chest and lungs, that proceed of hot causes, if it be continued taking for some time together. The leaves and roots work the same effects. They help much also in the excoriations of the bowels, and hardness of the mother, and in all hot and sharp diseases thereof. The juice drank in wine, or the decoction of them, do help women to a speedy and easy delivery. Pliny saith, that whosoever takes a spoonful of any of the Mallows, shall that day be free from all diseases that may come unto him; and that it is especially good for the falling-sickness. The syrup also and conserve made of the flowers, are very effectual for the same diseases, and to open the body, being costive. The leaves bruised, and laid to the eyes with a little honey, take away the imposthumations of them. The leaves bruised or rubbed upon any place stung with bees, wasps, or the like, presently take away the pain, redness, and swelling that rise thereupon. And Dioscorides saith, the decoction of the roots and leaves helps all sorts of poison, so as the poison be presently voided by vomit. A poultice made of the leaves boiled and bruised, with some bean or barley flower, and oil of Roses added, is an especial remedy against all hard tumours and inflammations, or imposthumes, or swellings of the privates, and other parts, and eases the pains of them; as also against the hardness of the liver or spleen, being applied to the places. The juice of Mallows boiled in old oil and applied, takes

away all roughness of the skin, as also the scurf, dandruff, or dry scabs in the head, or other parts, if they be anointed therewith, or washed with the decoction, and preserves the hair from falling off. It is also effectual against scalding and burnings, St. Anthony's fire, and all other hot, red, and painful swellings in any part of the body. The flowers boiled in oil or water (as every one is disposed) whereunto a little honey and allum is put, is an excellent gargle to wash, cleanse or heal any sore mouth or throat in a short space. If the feet be bathed or washed with the decoction of the leaves, roots, and flowers, it helps much the defluxions of rheum from the head; if the head be washed therewith, it stays the falling and shedding of the hair. The green leaves (saith Pliny) beaten with nitre, and applied, draw out thorn or prickles in the flesh.

The Marshmallows are more effectual in all the diseases before mentioned. The leaves are likewise used to loosen the belly gently, and in decoctions or clysters to ease all pains of the body, opening the strait passages, and making them slippery, whereby the stone may descend the more easily and without pain, out of the reins, kidneys, and bladder, and to ease the torturing pains thereof. But the roots are of more special use for those purposes, as well for coughs, hoarseness, shortness of breath and wheezing, being boiled in wine, or honeyed water, and drank. The roots and seeds hereof boiled in wine or water.

Charubel on Marshmallow

This little plant does not thrive very well in the Northern Counties of England. It gradually dwindles in size the further North it appears. My authorities say its localities are Salt-marshes, the Banks of Tidal Rivers, the South of England and Ireland. But I can find it plentifully distributed in places where there are no Salt-marshes, or Tidal Rivers. I have found the Common Marsh Mallow growing luxuriantly on the highway-sides in my native county, Montgomeryshire. This plant grows from two to three feet high, is branched and velvety in every part. The leaves are undivided, or three lobed; flowers; pale rose-colour, almost sessile in the axils of the upper leaves, or disposed in leafless spikes. This plant is so well known to country people generally, I need not waste time and occupy space with superfluous descriptions. Please note: the Cotton

Plant belongs to this same family; likewise, the showy Hollyhocks which are now naturalised in our gardens. One characteristic of the Mallow is its mucilage yield, a wellknown remedy for pectoral complaints such as old coughs, especially if accompanied by soreness. Country people are in the habit of making strong decoctions of this plant, mixed with honey, for these complaints, with good result. There is one item of value to state with respect to the Mallow family: that there is no poisonous species among them; hence they are destitute of any active properties when applied in an ordinary way. But I hope I can show you that the Mallow family in general, and the Marsh Mallow in particular, have active properties when applied as directed in these papers. I have already explained the whole healing process by this means, that no more need be said on these lines. I shall now proceed to notice those forms of disease for which the Marshmallow is the antidote. Hay fever, unusual discharge from the nose with frequent sneezing, attended with restlessness. It would cure influenza if applied in time.

The word for invocation is APH-HI-MOO. Should you, after all I have written, not know this plant, I feel confident that you would derive benefit by the use of this simple Invocation. The same holds with the other plants.

Medical use of Marshmallow

Marshmallow is sometimes used to form a protective layer on the skin and a lining for the digestive tract. The Marshmallow also contains chemicals that might decrease cough and fight infections.

Modern research

Marshmallow (*Althaea officinalis*) has long been cherished in traditional medicine for its soothing properties, particularly in treating coughs and respiratory issues. Modern research has begun to validate these age-old uses, shedding light on the pharmacological potential of this humble plant.

A comprehensive review published in *Complementary Medicine Research* examined both animal and clinical studies, confirming that extracts from *A. officinalis* effectively alleviate dry coughs. Interestingly, when combined with other herbal extracts like *Zataria multiflora*, *Zingiber officinalis* (ginger), or *Helix hedera* (ivy), the efficacy of Marshmallow increases, addressing various types of coughs. The study suggests that multiple mechanisms contribute to Marshmallow's expectorant and antitussive effects, making it a valuable component in herbal remedies for respiratory ailments.

Further investigations into the plant's phytochemistry have identified key constituents, including mucilage, phenolic acids, scopoletin, and flavonoids. These compounds are believed to contribute to Marshmallow's anti-inflammatory, antitussive, anti-infective, and antipyretic properties. Such findings confirm traditional applications and open avenues for integrating Marshmallow into modern therapeutic practices, especially in paediatric medicine for managing digestion and fever.

In essence, contemporary research is beginning to catch up with what herbalists have known for centuries, that Marshmallow offers a gentle yet effective approach to soothing respiratory discomforts and beyond. As we continue to explore its pharmacological profile, Marshmallow stands as a testament to the enduring wisdom found in traditional herbal medicine.

Personal experience

Marshmallow is a wonderful plant, full of kindness and generosity, and in my garden, she grows to impressive heights, not because she is entirely happy with where she is, but because she refuses to be anything less than magnificent. She would rather have more sun, but instead of sulking, she stretches upwards, reaching for the light with quiet determination.

Her leaves are irresistible, soft as the ears of a young Labrador pup, and no matter how many times you pass by, you will find yourself reaching out, just for the simple pleasure of touching them. She invites that connection and welcomes it, and that says a great deal about who she is.

Marshmallow works willingly with people, but she does not just soothe symptoms, she reminds you to look deeper. The roots of a problem matter, and if you do not address them, the issue will keep returning. True healing, she teaches, begins at the foundation, not just at the surface. Her roots, fittingly, are excellent for digestive troubles, and I have even used them to make a hay fever treatment for my long-suffering husband, one that worked an absolute treat.

Her presence is warm, steady, and wise, and I found her one of the easier plant spirits to contact. She feels deeply Venusian, but not in the airy, fleeting way of Libra; no, she is Venus in Taurus. Solid, grounded, patient. She holds knowledge like an old oak holds time, and when she speaks, it is with the kind of certainty that comes from experience. There is no rush with her, no urgency, just the steady assurance that healing comes when it is ready, when the roots are tended, and when the foundation is strong.

Meditative experience

She appeared to me as a middle-aged woman, full-bellied and warm, the kind of presence that belongs in the heart of a kitchen where something rich and fragrant is always on the boil. She smelled of honey and herbs, of fruit warmed by the sun, of damp earth after rain. There was flour dust on her hands, the kind that has kneaded a thousand loaves, and a patience in her eyes that spoke of seasons passing, of harvests gathered, of seeds tucked into the ground with the quiet promise of return.

Her gaze settled on me with knowing, a deep, steady wisdom that needed no words. She had tended, she had nurtured, she had given of herself over and over, and in doing so, she had become something vast, something eternal. She carried the weight of generations in the curve of her arms, in the way she moved with ease, as if every action, every stir of the pot, every turn of the soil, was part of some ancient, unbroken ritual.

She taught me that softness is not weakness but strength in its purest form. That to serve, to offer, to nourish is not a burden, but a joy, a way of being so deeply intertwined with the world that there is no distinction between giver and receiver. To give freely is to be fully alive, to allow the great wheel of life to turn as it should. She showed me that sacrifice is not loss, but transformation. That all things, in the end, return to where they came from, not as an ending, but as the next step in the endless, spiralling dance of creation.

She made me understand that to tend is to love, and to love is to live. That every moment spent in care, in stirring a pot, in planting a seed, in weaving a thread, is a spell, a prayer, a promise to the world that life continues. And when the time comes to return, to fold back into the soil and the roots and the growing things, it will not be an ending, but a homecoming.

Alchemical instructions

Make the tincture on Friday when the Moon is waxing and with the Moon in Taurus, but you can do it in any Earth sign. She likes you to sing her name when you are doing the tincture.

Charubel Name	Personal Name
APH-HI-MOO	SHASHINA
Charubel Sigil	Personal Sigil

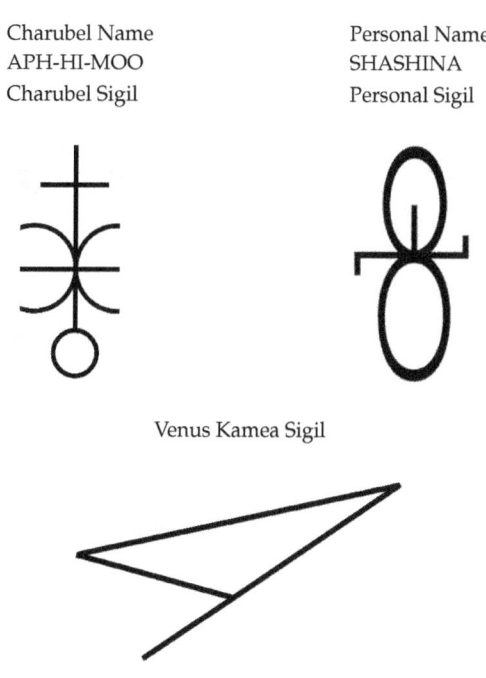

Venus Kamea Sigil

Shashina

Gentle
Kind
Softly spoken
Venus's daughter in pink veils falling
Sing to me as I sing to you
In service, you gain power
In giving, you can grow
Give thanks for all your sacrifice
It teaches you to know.

RO-VAM-HAL

THE BUTTERCUP
RANUNCULUS

Buttercup

Culpeper on Buttercup

Names

>Many are the names this furious biting herb has obtained; it is called frog's foot, from the Greek name barakion, crow-foot, gold-knobs, gold-cups, king's knob, baffiners, troil-flowers, polts, locket-goulions, and butter-flowers.
>
>Abundant are the sorts of this herb, and to describe them all would tire the patience of Socrates himself; therefore I shall only mention the most usual.

Description

>The most common crowfoot hath many darkgreen leaves, cut into divers parts, in taste biting and sharp, and blistering the tongue; it bears many flowers, and those of a bright resplendent yellow colour. I do not remember that I ever saw any thing yellower. Virgins in ancient times used to make powder of them to furrow bride beds. After the flowers come small heads, some spiked and rugged like a pineapple.

Place

> They grow very common everywhere; unless you turn your head into a hedge, you cannot but see them as you walk.

Time

> They flower in May and June, even till September.

Government and virtues

> This fiery and hot-spirited herb of Mars is no way fit to be given inwardly, but an ointment of the leaves of flowers will draw a blister, and may be so fitly applied to the nape of the neck, to draw back rheum from the eyes. The herb being bruised, and mixed with a little mustard, draws a blister as well and as perfectly as cantharides, and with far less danger to the vessels of urine, which cantharides naturally delight to wrong. I knew the herb once applied to a pestilential rising that was fallen down, and it saved life even beyond hope; it were good keeping an ointment and plaister of it, if it were but for that.

Charubel on Buttercup

THE BUTTERCUP (Ranunculus): Why this plant should be called Crowfoot is to me a puzzle; as the Native rightly interprets its name as Frog foot. It is not necessary that I should give a description of this plant, seeing it is one so familiar. All who may have wandered occasionally through the fragrant pasture lands of this country in the summer months. The children of rural districts are familiar admirers of the Buttercup. As I see this plant in my psychic condition, and from a soul point of view, it has a purple stem and yellow flower. The flower has three rows of petals. The centre contains a deep red Pistol, broad at the base, but tapers to a point at the top. Such then is the interior beauties of the little Buttercup; beauties are these which never fade. But it is not necessary all who read these words should see as I see, any more than that the many thousands of scientific facts should be realised by the multitude, individually; by the tardy process of primal experimentation, to derive from this and other plants their occult properties; or otherwise to transmit to others those properties, providing the one you desire to benefit be known to you.

The Crowfoot tribe are all more or less poisonous; they abound with an acrid juice, which is dangerous, more especially the Buttercup. This plant has been known to cause dangerous ulcers to develop on the hands from having handled them too freely; hence, such plants, however fascinating their flower might be, should not be held too caressingly. On the soul plane, Buttercup is yet even more poisonous. Although with this difference: you cannot on the soul plane give the patient this poison; hence if a person were to desire to injure another with the psychic poison, it would have no other effect than this; it would take from the person evil, to which it may be in sympathy, and this would disarm the person of a certain virus, by which it would prove a blessing and not a curse. Hence the laws on which all power connected with Psychic Botany are in direct opposition to the principles and practices of Black Magic; yes, for the connecting a person to a poisonous plant does not poison the individual; thereby, instead you take from that person the poison abounding in his nature to which the poisonous plant may be in sympathy. And further, an evil-disposed person cannot take an active part in these operations without receiving a personal good, and by such a practice, finally become a better man. Seeing that Buttercup has such properties on the soul plane, what are the evils that this little plant can heal? Those addicted to weeping, from no other cause than a consciousness of an indefinable gloom, a species of melancholia, a looking back, a longing for gone by scenes, an old home; departed friends; vanished pictures of hopeful days; anticipations unrealised; suicidal tendencies. One other physical evil for which this little plant is a psychopathic remedy: great heat in the face and forehead and inflamed eyes.

The word for invocation is RO-VAM-HAI.

Modern research

Buttercup (Ranunculus species) has long been admired for its bright, cheerful appearance, but beneath that sunny exterior lies a complex and potent chemistry. Modern pharmacological research has delved into the properties of various Ranunculus species, uncovering both their therapeutic potentials and toxicological risks.

Several Ranunculus species have been traditionally employed to treat ailments such as jaundice, oedema, malaria, asthma, pain, gout, and rheumatism. Contemporary studies have begun to validate these uses, revealing that extracts from these plants exhibit antibacterial, antiprotozoal, antioxidant, immunomodulatory, and anticancer properties. For instance, compounds isolated from Ranunculus muricatus have demonstrated significant antioxidant activity, while certain saponins from Ranunculus japonicus have shown promise in inhibiting cancer cell proliferation.

Despite these potential benefits, it's crucial to approach buttercup with caution. The plant contains toxins that can cause skin irritation and, if ingested, may lead to symptoms such as abdominal pain, diarrhoea, vomiting, and dizziness. These adverse effects underscore the importance of careful handling and thorough understanding before considering any medicinal application.

Personal experience

I cannot stop giggling at how much Charubel's experience of buttercup mirrors my own. You would think I would have learned by now, but no—I charged straight into my meditation with Buttercup before reading anything about it, naively assuming it must be a happy little Sun herb. I mean, it is bright yellow, cheerful-looking, and practically shines in the grass. What else could it possibly be?

Well. That was a BIG mistake.

Working with this plant turned out to be one of the most eye-opening experiences I have ever had, and not in the gentle, enlightening way. Buttercup is not an herb of the Sun; it is, beyond any shadow of a doubt, a Mars plant. And not the disciplined, orderly kind of Mars either. No, this is the scrappy, wild-eyed, pick-a-fight-in-a-tavern kind of Mars. It stings your hands with its juices, its stem is rough and jagged like it is actively trying to make you uncomfortable, and its personality? Aggressive. Utterly belligerent. It does not want to be tamed, and it makes that very, very clear.

Honestly, Buttercup feels less like a plant and more like an unruly spirit that will slap you across the face the moment you assume you know what it is about. Sweet and sunny? Absolutely not. More like a feral little warrior wrapped in golden deception, ready to prove you wrong at the first opportunity.

Meditational experience

He came to me as a soldier, not an officer, not a decorated general, but a corporal, rough and battle-worn, the kind who has seen too much and trusts too little. There was nothing refined about him, nothing polished. He had the air of a scrappy farm dog, the kind that patrols the land with teeth bared, convinced he could take your leg off before you even think about setting foot on his turf. And make no mistake—it was his turf. He was aggressively territorial, utterly uninterested in conversation, and made it very clear that he had no desire to work with me. No name. No sigil. No invitation. Just a cold, unwavering stare that told me, in no uncertain terms, to turn around and walk away. Of course, I can only speak from my own experience, but if nothing else, it proves a simple truth—not all plants want to be our friends. Some stand alone, untouched, unbothered, unwilling to yield even an inch of themselves. Charubel described Buttercup as attracting the dark moods of psychopaths, of those lost in depression and melancholy. I do not know if that is entirely true, but what I do know is that he carried himself with the reckless, unshakable certainty of something that truly believed it could take on the world and win.

If there ever comes a day when the earth burns and the cities crumble, when all that remains is ash and silence, I have no doubt that Buttercup and the cockroaches will be standing side by side, ruling whatever is left of the land.

RO-VA-MAL

Fuck off, he screamed
Brandishing bayonet and hat equally aggressively
Fuck you and all who come after
Tiny soldier of Mars
Screaming in the wind
Daring the rain to fall
Happy Face hiding Fangs and big balls
Come on you Bastards,
Come on!

HOO-VAH-MAH

THE ELDER

Elder

Culpeper on Elder

The juice of the leaves snuffed up into the nostrils purges the tunicles of the brain. A common tree with spreading branches and Oval sharp pointed leaves serrated about the edges. This is but an herb, every year dying with his stalks to the ground, and rising fresh every spring, and is like unto the elder both in form and quality, rising up with a square rough hairy stalk, four feet high, or more sometimes. The winged leaves are somewhat narrower than the elder, but else like them. The flowers are white with a dash of purple, standing in umbels, very like the elder also, but more sweet in scent, after which come small blackish berries, full of juice while they are fresh, wherein is small hard kernels, or seed, the root doth creep under the upper crust of the ground, springing in divers places, being of the bigness of one's finger or thumb sometimes.

Where to find it

In hedgerows and moist space places flowering time late spring. The berries are ripe in early autumn. The elder-tree groweth in hedges, being planted there to strengthen the fences and partitions of ground, and to hold the banks by ditches and water-courses.

Astrology

It is under the dominion of Venus.

Medicinal virtues

The bark, leaves, flowers and berries all have medicinal properties. The first shoots to appear boiled like asparagus and also the young leaves and stalks boiled in fat broth carry forth phlegm and choler. The middle and inward bark boiled in water and given in a drink works much more violently. The berries, either green or dry, expel the same humour. They were also given with good success to help dropsy. The bark of the root boiled in wine or drunk as a juice is more potent than the leaves or the fruit.

The juice of the root causes vomiting and purges the watery humours of dropsy. A decoction of the root modifies the mother's hardness if women sit thereon and open their veins and bring down their courses. The berries boiled in wine performed the same effect. The juice of the green leaves applied to hot inflammations of the eye assuages them. A decoction of berries in wine provokes urine. The leaves or flowers are distilled in the month of May, and if the legs are washed with it takes away ulcers and sores. The hands when washed with it helps the shaking of the man the palsy stops.

Charubel on Elder

The Elder tree is said to belong to the Honeysuckle family. Such classifications were found necessary for the study of botany as a science could never be effectively accomplished. Thus it was found necessary that there should be orders, classes, tribes or families. It does not necessarily follow those who have laid down, for our guidance, such and such rules and have described certain plants so that we may be able to identify them, that they should always be correct in their descriptive writings. Indeed I could contradict some of these writers were it worth my while to do so.

I was greatly surprised the other day, whilst reading a paragraph by Dr. Carpenter on the medical and other properties of the Elder Bark, to find him giving to this said bark an astringent property: "The bark is generally astringent; some species have been used for Tanning, and that of others has been employed in medicine for the same purpose, and with similar effects as Peruvian Bark". What I have to offer as a set-off to this is: That for the purpose of a brisk purgative and diuretic combined, I never found better than the decoction of the inner bark of the Elder. Is it possible that a purgative of so pronounced a character should be such an astringent? I have always considered an astringent that which binds together; the very reverse of laxative.

The Elder flourishes in damp smelly places, as well as along roadsides. It appears to possess the power of transmuting the corruptible into the incorruptible. It stands between the corruptible and us; it thus constitutes one of nature's filters. The word corruption is a relative term; for strictly speaking, truthfully, and philosophically, there is no corruption.

Corruption consists in too much of one element concentrated in one place. The fumes from a putrid carcass is corruption, but when that putrid mass is buried and a living plant imbibes its offensive fumes, it becomes transmuted into a living vegetable organism which represents the incorruptible.

Thus, the Elder tree absorbs the offensive effluvia emanating from stagnant pools and filthy sewers, thus changing them into life and loveliness.

The charms which this tree possesses are but few; nor is it ever looked on as an object of beauty, the odour it gives is anything but fragrant, nor are the odours from its flowers at all fascinating. But it yields a fruit that, if fully understood, is without a parallel in its several uses among the sick; its wine is equal to either Port or Sherry. Thus what may be lacking in the beautiful is more than compensated in the good and the useful.

The Elder is more plentifully distributed in the south of England than the north. I consider this tree a native of Britain, and existed in these parts long before that rupture took place, which cut off this land from the continent of Europe. Indeed I may confidently presume that it is one of the oldest fruit-bearing trees that this country possesses.

The influences of Venus in the sign Scorpio are allied to the Elder. I furnish you with the symbol of this tree's elemental powers and virtues. I hope such subjects as I am now giving may prove sufficiently interesting as to induce some to make it a part of their study: and that they may be led to see that there are more "secrets in heaven and earth" than modern scientists have ever dreamed in their philosophy. I shall here withdraw myself from the outer materialised tree and will look at this object on the soul plane.

The influences of the Psychic Elder appear to rotate at an inexpressible speed about its mystic centre, which I will, for convenience, designate the stem; at the same time, this stem becomes absolutely invisible! This invisible centre has several minor centres that branch off from the parent stem.

Each of these minor branches constitutes centres around which a proportionately smaller circle of influences revolves. These influences eventually become absorbed in mysterious vortices and are lost from view, at least from my view.

But after a few months, this whirl of atoms develops into a new phenomenon, consisting of new foliage, new flowers, and new clusters of berries.

I perceive the motion of this whirl, in the first instance, tends downwards towards the root part of the mystical stem, where it passes through a process of infiltration, when it afterwards ascends towards the extremities, having finished its mystic round.

Such is the order of that wonderful evolution on the soul plane before this tree is beheld on this outer plane; at least, such is what I realise on the inner plane. The seat of all force, the cause of every species of organic life is a vortex, and the centre of that vortex is a vacuum! It is here where dwells the motive energy; the God! Yes, it appears to me at this moment, that what I call a vacuity is the dwelling-place of Omnipotence!

In the next place, this tree on the soul plane, and as witnessed by me from a psychic standpoint, is of an intense dark purple colour. It, therefore, represents the feminine side of nature and is negative to all those matters with which it stands related.

I tell you one of heaven's grand mysteries: It is with the Negative side of Divinity that we have to do. It is the Mother's side of Deity, not the Father's side, the negative, and not the positive. The mother does not only embrace her offspring with the arms of her affection, but she feeds it from the breasts of her consolation. Thus it is that whilst we are the offsprings of nature, and are dandled on her knees, she bountifully meets our numerous and diversified wants with profusion from her exhaustless stores. In miniature, I discover in the Elder a very appropriate type of that phase of providence which I have been alluding to.

This tree is negative; hence it possesses properties, or instead attributes, as I view such organic forms as living agencies and not as a conglomeration of dead matter moved mechanically by some extraneous influences. So long as you look but at the outer form of the Elder, you will fail to appreciate those higher aspects, those more subtle virtues, which live immortally in this beautiful Symbol, which through the Divine aid I have exhumed from the buried past. Again: To what phase of human nature does this tree ally itself, so as to prove of value? The answer to this question arises spontaneously as I now write it: Persons of gross habits, and where there may be a tendency toward vices of a low and animal character. Such persons may be relieved from an intolerable burden, a burden which if hugged and carried will ultimately weigh its possessor down to the gates of death. "For he who sows to the flesh, shall of the flesh reap corruption." And this corruption is the second death.

The Elder tree, on the soul plane, is capable of absorbing those influences, which do fire the passions of those who are constitutionally exposed to such influences. It must be borne in mind that every species of vice originates in a disease that produces soul deformity. Whenever a person becomes abnormally developed in any phase of vice, that man or woman is the subject of a disease; for every disease in human nature, Nature has a cure. If our Philanthropists and Legislators were to pay attention to this; were half those funds, which now support Christian missions, devoted to the support of men who might be competent to receive and carry out these great truths which I could teach them, crime itself in a few generations might become extinct. But they will not heed any remarks from me; and they will go on with their hanging and imprisonments.

Here I offer freely a cure for one of the most prominent vices of this day: the vice of lust and animality. Turn your thoughts to this purple mother tree. She will absorb that pernicious poison which has become engendered in thy nature O man, and will convey it downwards where the poison becomes changed; it is there transmuted, and rendered capable of yielding to thee during the rest of thy life the beautiful flowers and fruits of rightness.

Some there are who may consider these teachings as being but the wild hallucinations of an enthusiast; one who may be supposed to have been long a denizen in the domain of imagination so as to have become intoxicated with those delusive dreams, which, like those fascinating exhalations which is said to have, at one time, ascended from the Pythian spring. But, what a sublime satisfaction it is to know that what the superficial thinkers, and writers, may understand by the epithet "imagination" as being equivalent to a vagary, the Occult Philosopher has made the very important discovery that this tabooed region of imagination is after all: the world, yes, the Universally Real.

When uninspired, the intellect alone moves within a radius of a very contracted circle. Within these limits, the unaided intellect gets bewildered by those numerous enigmas, which beset it on every hand.

After all those laborious researches, the testing and probing, and analytical siftings, when the diligent investigator is about to congratulate himself on his achievements, he may feel disposed to consider himself most fortunate, seeing he has attained to that long-looked for consummation. In the midst of all this, he finds he has a successor, a rival, whose discoveries on those same lines overturn the facts and theories of previous findings.

But the man whose intellect is illuminated with the true height of heaven has no call to fear that anyone who may take up these same subjects on these same lines will ever be in a position to say that what I have written is false. It is true, that another mind may appear on the scene at some future period, who may see more than I have seen, and who may express those lucid visions in loftier phrases. Yet, what I have written is written and will never be obliterated.

If the men and women of this generation choose to put these facts of mine to the test, I have no doubt, but results will prove satisfactory, providing the conditions be complied with.

The Occult Name of the Elder Tree is: HOO-VAH-MAH

Modern research

Elderberry has been traditionally used to treat colds and flu. Recent studies suggest that elderberry might shorten the duration and reduce the severity of cold and flu symptoms if taken within the first forty-eight hours of symptom onset. These effects are attributed to the high flavonoid content in elderberries, which may help mitigate oxidative stress and inflammation.

A comprehensive review highlighted that elderberry extracts exhibit antiviral activity against influenza viruses, potentially reducing the duration and severity of flu symptoms. Further studies have demonstrated that elderberry extracts possess antiviral activity against the modified vaccinia virus Ankara (MVA), suggesting a broader spectrum of antiviral effects.

Additionally, research has indicated that elderberry extracts can inhibit the replication of SARS-CoV-2, the virus responsible for COVID-19, highlighting its potential as a complementary therapeutic option.

Personal experience

Working with the Elder tree was not like working with a single being, but three distinct and separate presences, each shifting with the turning of the year. She was the Three in One, the embodiment of transition and transformation. Just as I cannot think of her without thinking of Hekate, mistress of the crossroads, keeper of three secret names—Aktiophis, Erishkagel, Neboutosouleth—I cannot work with her without feeling each of her faces step forward in turn.

The first lady

This was the Elder in spring, bright-eyed and wild, her branches heavy with delicate white blossoms, tiny snowflakes scattered across wide, open hands. Her scent was sharp and acrid, sweet but with that unmistakable bite of cat pee, a perfume both inviting and challenging. She spoke of growth and increase, of bursting into being, of flinging oneself headlong into life. She was Venus in Aries, bold, strident, confident. No gentle maiden, but a force of awakening, the sheer exultation of motion and momentum.

I tinctured her in vodka, sweetened with honey, and every time I take a drop, it sings of spring, of birdsong carried on crisp morning air, of green voices rising in a chorus of joy, of the raw, intoxicating thrill of rebirth.

The second lady

She came in the heat of summer, her blossoms now rich, heavy berries, dark and bursting with promise. She was deeper, stronger, more grounded, her perfume lower and warmer, rich with the scent of ripeness. She spoke of sex and reproduction, of the earth's quiet and knowing ways. She taught me to listen—to the wind, to the birds, to the plants conspiring together to spread their seeds. She was Venus in Scorpio, though I suspect she hovered on the cusp of Sagittarius, for there was laughter in her wisdom, a mischievous joy in her lessons.

From her berries, I made syrup, thick and dark, and a small tincture in vodka, stained a luminous purple. She is the richness of late summer, the heat of bodies moving together, the laughter that comes from deep in the belly.

The third lady

Then came winter, and with it, the third face of Elder. Her branches stood bare against the cold, her bark rough and weathered, no longer the giver of fruit and bloom. She was slow and sharp, and when I reached for her, she let me know, this is not your time. There was no warmth in her now, no soft edges, only the stillness of deep knowledge and the weight of sleep not to be disturbed. She would not give me anything for tincture, would not entertain my presence for long. She was powerful, but she had no time for me, and I knew better than to push.

I will not work with her again. Not because I do not respect her, but because I do. Some things are not meant to be touched, and some spirits, even when they share their other faces willingly, prefer to be left alone when the world turns dark.

Charubel Name: HOO-VAH-MAH
Personal names:
Spring: No name, only the smell
Vathne—The Berry tree (summer tree)
Winter tree—No name

Charubel's Sigil   Personal Sigil   Venus Kamea

Vathne

The three in one
With berries dripping
The memory of lace flowers in my mind
Of spring's first fancy
Of wings with fruit ascending
Of Hekate's three faces
Found in one
Of joy in the growth
Of joy in the fruiting
And then to sleep deeply
Undisturbed!

A
I
A

THE BRAMBLE

Bramble

Culpeper on Bramble

Name

It is also called blackberry bush, and is so well known that it needs no description; its virtues are as follows.

Government and virtues

It is a plant of Venus in Aries. You have directions at the latter end of the book for the gathering of all herbs, plants, &c. The reason why Venus is so prickly is because she is in the house of Mars. The buds, leaves, and branches, while they are green, are of good use in the ulcers and putrid sores of the mouth and throat, and for the quinsey; and likewise to heal other fresh wounds and sores: but the flowers and fruit unripe are very binding; they are also profitable for the bloody flux and lasks [menstural bleeding], and a fit remedy for spitting of blood. Either the decoction or powder of the root, being taken, is good to break or drive forth gravel and the stone in the reins or kidneys. The leaves and brambles, as well green as dry, are good lotions for sores in the mouth or secret parts; the decoction of them and of the dried branches doth much bind the belly, and is good for too much flowing of women's courses; the berries or the flowers are a powerful remedy against the poison of the most venomous serpents as well drunk, as outwardly applied, and help the sores of the fundament, and the piles; the juice of the berries, mixed with juice of mulberries, do bind more effectually, and help fretting and eating sores and ulcers where-soever. The distilled water of the branches, leaves, and flowers, or fruit, is very pleasant in taste, and very effectual in fevers and hot distempers of the body, head, eyes, and other parts, and for all the purposes aforesaid. The leaves boiled in lye, and the head washed therewith heal the itch, and the running sores thereof, and make the hair black. The powder of the leaves strewed on cancers and running ulcers doth wonderfully help to heal them. Some condensate, the juice of the leaves, and some juice of the berries, to keep for their use all the year, for the purposes aforesaid.

Charubel on Bramble

There is no commentary on Bramble in Charubel's Grimoire.

Modern research

Blackberries are teeming with antioxidants, particularly anthocyanins, which not only bestow their deep hue but also combat oxidative stress in the body. This action helps neutralise free radicals, potentially reducing the risk of chronic diseases.

Beyond their sweet taste, blackberries exhibit antimicrobial properties. Studies have shown that compounds extracted from the fruit can inhibit the growth of certain bacteria and fungi, suggesting a role in supporting the body's defences against infections.

Traditionally, blackberry leaves and roots have been used to treat digestive issues like diarrhoea and dysentery. The astringent properties of tannins present in these parts of the plant are believed to be responsible for these effects, offering a natural remedy for gastrointestinal discomfort.

The anti-inflammatory properties of blackberries have been recognised in both traditional and modern medicine. They have been used to alleviate pain and swelling, providing a natural option for those seeking relief from inflammation-related conditions

Personal experience

I set out deliberately to work with Bramble—not just because she has such an odd, almost contradictory nature, but because there were hundreds of them in the fields where we lived, twisting and tangling their way across the land. And, if I am honest, I was also keen to test an old tale told to me by a farmer, one that had stayed with me, whispering in the back of my mind.

I understand exactly why Culpeper called her Venus in Aries; she is thorned and bloomed, with sweet fruit and sharp bites. But there is something else in her too, something slow, patient, and relentless. To me, she also carries the weight of Capricorn. She builds beneath herself, weaving a cage of near impenetrable thorns, a fortress as much as a snare. She is a contradiction—a delicate rose-like flower in spring, a cascade of green, red, and blackberries in autumn, luscious and tempting. And yet, she is utterly ruthless. There is not a soul alive who has not paid for her fruit with bloodied hands and scratched-up legs. She demands a price.

The farmer who told me the tale was convinced Bramble was an evil plant, a thing of the devil, a killer of sheep, feeding off their corpses. The idea that something so beautiful could also be a predator intrigued me. So, as I do, I went out to sit, to listen, to see what she would say. What I got was not what I expected.

She was deep—deep-deep—her energy reminding me of Kharon, the psychopomp, the ferryman who carries souls across the Styx. She would answer any question, but always for a price. And I paid. I gave her offerings, urine, liver bought just for her, gifts she accepted in the quiet, patient way of something that has always known its worth.

She spoke of the great web of existence, the parasitic nature of reality, of how nothing truly gives without taking. She showed me the damage humans are doing to the soil, how we strip it bare and then curse the things that must adapt to survive in its ruin. I asked her about the sheep. Was it true? Was she a killer?

She answered, and she did not lie. Yes, she takes meat, but only when the land demands it. The farmer had worked the field without laying down fertiliser, leaving the earth starved of nutrients. So she took what was needed.

Later, I did my research, and there it was—scientific evidence that Bramble does take animals when the soil is depleted. It is no accident that her thorns curve slightly backward. Once something gets caught, every struggle only tightens the hold. The body dies, decomposes, and the nitrates feed her roots. A perfect cycle. A perfect exchange.

She is neither good nor evil. She is simply Bramble, beauty and trap, sweetness and teeth, a creature of necessity, as all things in nature are.

Meditational experience

She came to me as a filthy beggar, wrapped in rags crusted with earth, her face streaked with the grime of a life spent too close to the bones of the world. In her hand, she carried a stick, something gnarled and dark, like a blackthorn rod, and she used it, jabbing me sharply whenever she decided I was being particularly slow to understand.

She spat when she spoke, a guttural and wet punctuation to her words. She reeked, of damp soil and rotting things, of the sharp tang of decay, of filth ground so deep into flesh that it had become part of her. There was nothing gentle about her, nothing warm or welcoming. She was the embodiment of what we prefer to ignore, what we pretend does not exist, the refuse of life, the unavoidable end that waits beneath all things green and growing.

I found her intimidating, unsettling, and entirely worth the pursuit. She was wisdom carved from the marrow of the earth, and she did not waste time on pleasantries. To sit with her was to be prodded, pushed, and forced to see what I would rather not.

And my poor legs? They have never forgiven me.

Alchemical work

I tinctured her leaves in the spring and made a decoction of her stem. I did not want to go for her roots as she would have extracted a price for this, one that was too high. I did not tincture her fruits: in Wales, we eat Blackberry pie and make jam in the autumn, so I did not feel I needed more exposure to her.

Charubel name:
No name in Grimoire
Personal Sigil

Personal Name
AIA
Venus Kamea Sigil

AIA

Green girded blade barked
Grasping, pulling, mewling, killing
Underworld seeker
Asking a price
For shiny baubles all squishy with juice
A coin for the traveller, some meat for the bones
And I will tell you the stories of Webs and of Stones.

MAUDE

LUNGWORT

Lungwort

Culpeper on Lungwort

This is a kind of moss, that grows on sundry sorts of trees, especially oaks and beeches, with broad, greyish, tough leaves diversly folded, crumpled, and gashed in on the edges, and some spotted also with many small spots on the upper-side. It was never seen to bear any stalk or flower at any time.

Government and virtues

Jupiter seems to own this herb. It is of great use to physicians to help the diseases of the lungs, and for coughs, wheezings, and shortness of breath, which it cures both in man and beast. It is very profitable to put into lotions that are taken to stay the moist humours that flow to ulcers, and hinder their healing, as also to wash all other ulcers in the privy parts of a man or woman. It is an excellent remedy boiled in beer for broken-winded horses.

Note from Sian

Now, I have an issue with Culpeper's description of Lungwort. Firstly, he is describing a moss here, not a plant, and he clearly says that the plant does not give any stalk or flower, which is untrue of Pulmonaria. It is entirely possible that Culpeper made a bit of a mix-up regarding Lungwort in his grand herbal classifications. Given his penchant for assigning planetary rulerships based on appearance and function, it would not be surprising if he mistakenly lumped together Lobaria pulmonaria, the Lungwort lichen, and Pulmonaria officinalis, the Lungwort plant. And, to be fair, at a glance, it is an easy enough mistake to make.

Both are tied to the lungs, have a spotted, irregular look resembling diseased tissue (a classic case of the Doctrine of Signatures in action), and have long been used in folk medicine to support respiratory health. However, while Pulmonaria officinalis is a soft-leaved, flowering herb, Lobaria pulmonaria is a crusty, moss-like lichen that clings to old trees like something out of deep time, but sounds much closer to the description that Culpeper gave.

Since Culpeper was working in an era where plants were often identified by their broader associations rather than strict botanical taxonomy, it is entirely possible that his writings on Lungwort blurred the lines between the two. If he did, it would not be the first time herbalists have conflated similar-looking species—especially when both share a history of medicinal use.

The irony, of course, is that Lobaria pulmonaria has been found to be an incredible indicator of air quality and ecological health, while Pulmonaria officinalis is an actual medicinal herb still used for lung ailments today. One clings to the bark of ancient trees, speaking of the purity of forgotten landscapes; the other thrives in shaded gardens, offering its soft leaves as a remedy.

I would put Lungwort as Jupiter in Gemini because of its associations with the lungs, but also because of the need of breath for communication.

Charubel on Lungwort

Charubel has no commentary on this plant.

Modern research

Lungwort (Pulmonaria officinalis) has been used for centuries as a healer of the lungs, and now modern research is finally catching up with what traditional herbalists have known all along. Rich in mucilage, astringents, and minerals—particularly silica—Lungwort supports and strengthens delicate tissues, making it particularly suited to inflammatory conditions that weaken the structural integrity of the lungs.

Lungwort's primary strength lies in its ability to support respiratory health. It has long been used for conditions such as nasal congestion, coughs, influenza, bronchitis, laryngitis, and even tuberculosis. But where it truly shines is in more advanced cases, where lung function is severely compromised due to chronic inflammation and tissue damage. Contemporary herbalist Matthew Wood describes Lungwort as particularly effective in cases where lung structure has deteriorated, offering a stabilising and restorative influence.

Recent research is beginning to validate these traditional uses, particularly in relation to chronic obstructive pulmonary disease (COPD) and inflammatory lung conditions. Studies highlight Lungwort's ability to soothe, repair, and strengthen lung tissue, making it a potential ally for those suffering from long-term respiratory distress. Its high mucilage content coats and protects the airways, while its anti-inflammatory properties help to reduce irritation and swelling in the respiratory system.

While Lungwort is best known for its lung-supporting abilities, it also extends its healing touch to the digestive and urinary systems:

Digestive Health: Its mucilage soothes and coats the gastrointestinal tract, helping with conditions like ulcers, intestinal bleeding, diarrhoea, and haemorrhoids. At the same time, its astringent properties help to tone and strengthen the tissues, making it useful in cases of chronic digestive distress.

Kidney & Urinary Tract Health: Lungwort has antibacterial properties that assist in managing inflamed or infected kidneys and urinary tracts. Its toning effect on kidney and bladder tissues makes it useful in cases of infections, blood in the urine, and urinary incontinence.

Maria Leporatti's research into European medicinal plants reinforces what herbalists have known for generations, listing Lungwort as an emollient, antitussive, expectorant, antimicrobial, diuretic, depurative, antilithiatic, and anti-inflammatory—a powerhouse of healing potential for both respiratory and urinary conditions.[13]

Lyubov Dyshlyuk's work expands on this, highlighting Lungwort's rich antioxidant profile and its potential role in anti-ageing, cataract prevention, and improving blood flow to the retina. With such a high concentration of polyphenols (86.96%), flavonoids (75.47%), and proanthocyanidins (51.25%), it is no wonder Lungwort has earned its place as a medicinal staple.[14]

And yet, as always, modern science attributes these effects purely to its chemical components, as if the plant itself does not exist beyond its molecules. There is no recognition of its presence, spirit, or wisdom woven into its form, just the dry data of percentages and compounds.

But we who work with the plants know better. Lungwort is not just a collection of polyphenols, it is a living, breathing ally, one that has been tending to human lungs for centuries and will continue to do so, long after the studies are forgotten.

Personal experience

Lungwort is one of those plants that demands attention, not in an ostentatious way, but through its sheer presence. There is something undeniably striking about it, with its speckled leaves that look like diseased lungs, a visual nudge that medieval healers took as a clear sign of its purpose. It was used for coughs, asthma, and all manner of lung complaints long before anyone had the scientific evidence to back it up. The name alone tells you exactly what it is for.

Here in Wales, Lungwort is one of the first plants to bloom, a herald of spring pushing its way through damp earth with vivid pink and purple flowers. It thrives in the cool, shadowed corners, the kind of damp, low-light places that define the Welsh landscape. Hildegard von Bingen, the twelfth century German herbalist, praised its virtues, not just for humans but for livestock too, particularly in treating swollen lungs.

---

[13] Maria Laura Leporatti and Svetlana Ivancheva, "Traditional Phytotherapy of the Villagers in the Middle Valnerina (Umbria, Central Italy)," *Journal of Ethnopharmacology* 87, nos. 2–3 (2003).

[14] Lyubov S. Dyshlyuk et al., "Optimization of Extraction of Polyphenolic Compounds from Medicinal Lungwort (Pulmonaria officinalis L.)," *Journal of Pharmaceutical Research International* 32, no. 24 (2020).

Packed with mucilage, astringents, and minerals, particularly silica, it is a plant designed to soothe, repair, and strengthen.

Lungwort's reputation as a healer of the lungs is well earned. It has been used for nasal congestion, coughs, influenza, bronchitis, laryngitis, and even tuberculosis. In cases of severe respiratory distress, it is said to help rebuild lung tissue, supporting those struggling to breathe.

For me, working with Lungwort has been deeply personal. Growing up in Wales, where coal mining shaped both the land and the people, I have always been surrounded by the echoes of industry. My grandfather and great-grandfather, like so many others, suffered from pneumoconiosis, black lung, from years of inhaling coal dust. Respiratory disease was not just something you read about in books; it was in the stories of my family, in the air itself. Lungwort was one of my Gran's household remedies. She grew it in abundance, using it in teas, and surprisingly even as a smoked herb, a kind of makeshift tobacco for easing congestion.

When I began working with Lungwort myself, I felt an urge to deepen that connection through the Charubel method, tying my work with the plant to my own roots. I took cuttings from my Gran's old house.

Gran's Lungwort

Lungwort has always felt like a bridge between the past and the present, between breath and memory. The plant I took from my gran's garden had long, spotted leaves and delicate white flowers, but there was nothing fragile about her. She was sturdy, deeply rooted, and anchored in a way that felt both reassuring and determined.

When I first sat with her, breathing in her essence, I could feel her working, opening up not just my lungs but my heart centre too. It was not just about drawing in air; it was about really feeling it, noticing how it reached into the deepest parts of me. There was a quiet clarity in that moment, a realisation that breath is not just about survival, it is about connection.

And then, there was my Gran. The spirit of the plant seemed to shift, to take on something of her presence. Maybe it was because of the link between them, her garden, her care, the way she had always spoken of Lungwort with a quiet reverence. Or maybe it was something deeper, something woven into the very essence of the plant.

My Gran had suffered with her breathing all her life. She was the only one of fifteen siblings who did not go into service, simply because her body would not allow it. And yet, she was strong in her own way, rooted, resilient, just like the plants she grew in her garden.

She used to talk about how the land had to heal, how it had suffered just as the people had. Our family came from the Rhondda Valley, coal-mining country, where the air smelt of sulphur from the coke ovens, thick and acrid, clinging to the back of the throat. It was not just the air that bore the scars, but the land itself. The Welsh poet Max Boyce once sang of it in *Rhondda Grey*, describing how the valleys, once green and full of life, had been stained with coal dust, taking on a grey, lifeless hue. The mines took so much, not just from the land but from the bodies and spirits of the people who worked them. Breathing itself had been a struggle, not just for her but for so many.

But Lungwort, this unassuming plant with its freckled leaves and steadfast roots, spoke of recovery. It reminded me that healing is possible, not just for a single person but for the land itself. Working with her, I felt a deep sense of hope. The damage we have done, to ourselves, to the air, to the soil, can be undone. But only if we stop seeing the world as something to use and start seeing it as something we are a part of. A community, not a playground.

Every time I sit with Lungwort, I feel that message settle into me. It is not just about my breath, or my Gran's, or the breath of those who came before. It is about all of us, about the air we share, the land we walk on, and the healing that is still possible, if we listen.

Meditation

She comes as my Gran, tiny, white-haired, fragile-looking, yet as steady as the earth itself. She allows me to sit at her knee, just as I did when I was small, and as we talk, she strokes my head, her fingers moving in time with my breath. Slow, measured, knowing.

With each touch my breathing deepens, my ribs widening to take in the cold, crisp air. It is not just cool, it is deep-down, bone-deep cold, sinking into my chest, filling every space, reaching down to my toes in a bright, tingling energy. It spreads through me, awakening something long-forgotten, something vast and old.

She speaks then, her voice soft, steady, carrying the weight of memory. She talks of black rivers, thick and lifeless, winding their way through broken land. She tells me of the gaping wounds in the hills, deep cuts left behind where men carved out the coal, their sweat and breath the price paid for fire and progress. She speaks of the miners, their bodies bent and dust-laden, their wages counted not in coin but in the shortening of their days. Payment for the coal taken not from the ground but from their lungs. Their lives ending in gasping, clawing for breath, as though the earth itself had come to reclaim the air stolen from its depths.

And then, her voice shifts, not to anger, not to blame, but to warning, to wisdom. She tells me this is how it could end for all of us, if mankind does not learn, if we do not listen, if we do not change. But her words are not sharp, not spoken in punishment, only in care. She soothes, as she always did, her fingers still moving in time with my breath. She tells me there is still time, that the earth is patient, and that healing is possible. That if we choose, if we wake, if we see the world as something to be cherished rather than consumed, we can put it right.

And as she speaks, the cold air moves deeper still, not just filling me but changing me. I breathe in, and with it, I take her wisdom, her knowing, her quiet certainty that it is not too late. I breathe out, and in that breath is a promise.

It was only later that I realised I was not given a name. It was a plant I knew in form and feeling but not in words. Perhaps that was because, in that moment, she was something more. A presence, a blending, a meeting of spirit and memory. The plant had taken on something of my Gran, or perhaps my Gran had woven herself into the plant. They were one and the same to me, breath and roots entwined. And so, in honour of that, I gave her my Gran's name. The name that carries love, warmth, and the soft rhythm of her breath—Maude. Because to me, she was never just a memory, never just a whisper of the past. She was hands in the earth and a presence in the stillness. She was comfort and knowing, strength wrapped in tenderness. And now she is here, rooted in green, in leaf and flower, in the deep breath that fills my lungs. She is Maude. She always was. She always will be.

Personal Sigil

Jupiter Kamea Sigil

Note

To say I was surprised by the shape of the kamea sigil would be putting it far too lightly, my gast was well and truly flabbered. I've always felt a deep, undeniable force in naming Lungwort after my gran, as if the act itself wove their spirits together. But seeing the sigil take shape on the Jupiter Kamea was something else entirely. There it was, clear as day, the merging of two energies so bound that untangling them was impossible. The moment it appeared, the weight of it hit me, and I sat there, tears spilling, utterly overwhelmed, Maude would have told me to "man up".

Maude

    Fae-like and free
    Silver-haired whispering soul of the land
    Gran's hand in my hair deeply missed
    Breathe in, breathe out
    Breath catching in the chest
    Feeding the pain of the land and the body
    Old men of thirty carrying the weight of the world
    In sacks on their backs
    Open your lungs and breathe
    Open your minds and see
    And in seeing
    Take action
    And live

LLYS

EYEBRIGHT

Eyebright

Culpeper on Eyebright

Description

Common Eyebright is a small low herb, rising up usually but with one blackish green stalk a span high or not much more, spread from the bottom into sundry branches, whereon are small and almost round, yet pointed, dark green leaves, finely snipped about the edges, two always set together, and very thick: at the joints with the leaves, from the middle upward, come forth small white flowers, steeped with purple and yellow spots, or stripes; after which follow small round heads, with tiny seed therein. The root is long, small, and thready at the end.

Place

It grows in meadows and grassy places in this country.

Government and virtues

It is under the sign of the Lion, and Sol claims dominion over it. The juice or distilled water of eye-bright, taken inwardly in white wine or broth, or dropped into the eyes, for divers days together, helps all infirmities of the eyes that cause dimness of sight. Some make conserve of the flowers to the same effect. Using any of these methods also helps a weak brain or memory. This tunned up with solid beer, that it may work together, and drank; or the powder of the herb mixed with sugar, a little mace, and fennel-seed, and drank, or eaten in broth; or the said powder made into an electuary with sugar, and taken, has the same powerful effect to help and restore the sight decayed through age. Arnoldus de Ville Nova says, it has restored sight to them that have been blind a long time before.[15]

Charubel on Eyebright

Charubel has no commentary on Eyebright.

Mythology and folklore

In ancient folklore, carrying Eyebright flowers was said to enhance psychic abilities or reveal hidden truths. Often called "Christ's Eyes" or "Christ's Sight", Eyebright has long been revered not only for its resemblance to the human eye but also for its traditional use in treating eye ailments.

Eyebright's history goes far beyond eye health. In the Middle Ages, it was combined with tobacco to help relieve bronchial colds, and in the Elizabethan era, it was famously brewed into Eyebright Ale, believed to improve eyesight.[16]

Modern research

This small, delicate herb, with flowers that look like tiny eyes, has long been used to support eye health and improve vision. Packed with phytonutrients that specifically target eye discomfort and inflammation.

---

[15] Nicholas Culpeper, *The complete herbal* (anboco, 2016).
[16] C. T. Leffler et al., "Enduring influence of elizabethan ophthalmic texts of the 1580s: bailey, grassus, and guillemeau," *Open Ophthalmol J* 8 (2014), https://doi.org/10.2174/1874364101408010012.

Modern research has recently taken a closer look at Eyebright. One study shows that the biological effects of *E. officinalis L.* depend on both the concentration and the solvent used for extraction. Ethanol and ethyl acetate extracts demonstrated beneficial effects, reducing the expression of pro-inflammatory cytokines (IL-1β, IL-6, TNF-α, which stand for Interleukin 1 beta, Interleukin 6, and Tumour Necrosis factor Alpha) and the anti-inflammatory cytokine IL-10 in human corneal cells after twenty-four hours. These findings suggest that ethanol and ethyl acetate extracts of *E. officinalis L.* may be effective as supplementary therapies for eye disorders.[17]

Rich in aucubin, this herb delivers potent anti-inflammatory effects, making it ideal for soothing tired, irritated eyes. Its natural tannins act as astringents, drying secretions and calming inflammation, perfect for issues like conjunctivitis or blepharitis. Additionally, Eyebright contains quercetin, a flavonoid that helps reduce histamine release and eases hay fever symptoms like watery, itchy eyes. For styles, its caffeic acid provides antiseptic properties, while antioxidants support the absorption of vitamins A and C, essential for maintaining overall eye health. Its mineral content, including zinc, copper, and selenium, even helps prevent cataracts.

Personal experience

Eyebright comes as an old man, quiet and patient, his presence steady, his words measured. He did not rush to teach, did not flood me with visions or overwhelm me with revelation. Instead, he guided gently, letting me come to understanding in my own time.

He told me that we do not perceive the world as it is. We see it through the lens of our own experience, fears, and assumptions. It is a kind of blindness, subtle yet profound, shaping everything we think we know. We look, but we do not always see. We listen, but we do not always hear. We assume, without realising how much we are missing.

---

[17] Roman Paduch et al., "Assessment of Eyebright (Euphrasia Officinalis L.) Extract Activity in Relation to Human Corneal Cells Using In Vitro Tests," [Assessment of Eyebright (Euphrasia Officinalis L.) Extract Activity in Relation to Human Corneal Cells Using In Vitro Tests.] *Balkan Medical Journal* 2014, no. 1 (January 2014), https://doi.org/10.5152/balkanmedj.2014.8377, https://doi.org/10.5152/balkanmedj.2014.8377.

He asked me to think of the bees, their world painted in, a spectrum beyond our reach. To them, flowers hold hidden patterns leading them to nectar. To us, those markings do not exist, yet they are there, written across the petals in colours beyond our sight. He spoke of bats, hearing the world in echoes, mapping space with sound while we stumble blindly in the dark. Of hounds who scent a story on the wind, following invisible trails we could never hope to track.

We like to believe we see the full picture, that what we perceive is truth, but we are bound by the limits of our form. We can only see, hear, feel, and experience what our bodies allow, and that is only a fraction of what exists. Our understanding of the world is shaped by these constraints, a narrow window through which we glimpse only part of the vast, endless reality surrounding us.

But Eyebright was not trying to make me feel small or insignificant. His lesson was not one of despair, but of expansion. If we accept that our perception is limited, we can learn to question it. If we recognise that we do not see the whole truth, we can start searching for more. This is not just about vision, not just about clarity—it is about connection. To see the world more clearly is to step into it fully, to engage with it as it truly is, rather than as we expect it to be. It is to see people beyond our assumptions, to meet them where they are, not where we imagine them to be.

Eyebright teaches gently, but his lesson lingers. He does not force clarity upon us; he invites us to seek it. And if we listen, if we let ourselves be open, we might just find that the world is far more than we ever imagined.

The name I received was Llys.

Meditation

He comes as an old man, wise and wrinkled, his skin traced with the lines of time. His eyes are blue, blue like the sky on a winter's day, like water so deep it holds its own stories. He watches, unhurried, knowing.

"You think you see the world," he says, voice soft as falling leaves, "but do you?"

His question lingers, settling into the spaces between heartbeats. We move through our days believing our eyes show us truth, that our ears bring us all the music of the world, that what we touch is all that is real. But we are creatures bound by our form, wrapped in senses that only let in fragments of something far greater.

He speaks of the owl, its vision cutting through the darkness where we see nothing but shadow. Of the bat, hearing the world in echoes, moving through unseen landscapes of sound. Of the hound, reading scent like words in the air, tracing footsteps long since gone. Each creature believing in its own truth, each unaware of the ways others perceive what they cannot.

And so, he says, we are the same. We take our sight, our hearing, our understanding, and we shape the world from it. We call our perception truth, forgetting that it is only ever part of the story.

How often do we do this in life? How often do we look at someone and believe we know them, when we have only seen the surface? How often do we assume, when we have not listened deeply enough to hear what is truly there?

Truth is not a single thing, not fixed or whole. It shifts, bends, reveals itself only in pieces. What we know today may change when seen from another angle, when heard in a different voice, when touched with hands willing to feel rather than grasp.

"You do not have to know everything", Eyebright murmurs, his blue eyes holding something vast, something endless. "You only have to remember that there is always more."

Breathe that in. Let it settle in your bones, in the spaces between your thoughts. Let yourself be open, not just to what you can see, but to what you cannot. The world is wider than your senses, deeper than your knowing.

And wisdom comes, not from certainty, but from the willingness to keep looking.

Personal Sigil   Sol Kamea Sigil

Llys

Beauty seen and Beauty known
Are different things
Truth to one is a lie to another
Seeing is not believing
Appearances are deceiving
When you do not see it all
The world is far bigger than we think it is
Perception needs to change
To give a new perspective
To know that you do not know
Is wisdom beyond reckoning.

A R Y R

COLUMBINE

Columbine

Culpeper on Columbine

These are so well known, growing almost in every garden, that I think I may save the expense of time in writing a description of them.

Time

They flower in May, and abide not for the most part when June is past, perfecting their seed in the mean time.

Government and virtues

It is also an herb of Venus. The leaves of columbines are commonly used in lotions with good success for sore mouths and throats; Tragus saith, that a drachm of the seed taken in wine with a little saffron, openeth obstructions of the liver, and is good for the yellow-jaundice, if the party after the taking thereof be laid to sweat well in his bed; the seed also taken in wine causeth a speedy delivery of women in child-birth: if one draught suffice not, let her drink a second, and it will be effectual. The Spaniards use to eat a piece of the root hereof fasting, many days together, to help them when troubled with the stone in the kidneys.

Charubel on Columbine

There is no commentary on Columbine in Charubel.

Mythology and folklore

Columbine or Aquilegia first appeared in recorded garden history through Hildegard of Bingen, who cultivated it at Rupertsberg and used it in tinctures to treat fever and sore throats. Its distinctive form made it a favourite for manuscript illustration, and it appears frequently in medieval breviaries and psalters across Europe. A quick search will turn up plenty of examples.

Those delicate, fluttering petals were unmistakably bird-like: an association that stuck. Columbine comes from the Latin *columba*, meaning dove, linking the flower to the Holy Spirit. Meanwhile, *aquila*, meaning eagle, lends a more dramatic interpretation. The plant has no shortage of folk names, many of them rooted in British tradition. I've always known it as granny's bonnet, but in different parts of the country, you might hear it called boots-and-shoes, Dolly's bonnet, lion's herb, rags and tatters, or widow's weeds, among many others.

Wild columbines are largely blue, the colour of royal mourning in France, which led to their association with widows and, by extension, the sorrows of Mary. The idea travelled, as folklore does. And if that weren't enough, columbine was also known as *herba leonis* due to the peculiar belief that lions found it a delicious snack (don't ask). As a result, the plant took on yet another layer of meaning, and carrying the flowers, or even rubbing some of the sap into your hands, was thought to instil courage and fearlessness, qualities befitting the king of beasts.

Modern research

Modern research into the medicinal properties of Aquilegia species has uncovered some fascinating potential benefits, though any practical application needs to be approached with care, this is a plant with a known toxic side.

Studies on Aquilegia pubiflora have shown that its extracts have antimicrobial effects against a range of pathogenic bacteria, including

Bacillus subtilis, Klebsiella pneumoniae, Staphylococcus epidermidis, Pseudomonas aeruginosa, and Escherichia coli. The level of effectiveness varied, but the results suggest that the plant may have potential in developing treatments for bacterial infections.

Research into Aquilegia sibirica, a species used in traditional Mongolian medicine, has highlighted its antifungal properties. Extracts from the plant have been found to inhibit the growth of certain fungal pathogens, making it a candidate for future antifungal treatments. The presence of compounds such as chlorogenic acid and caffeic acid may play a role in these effects, adding to the plant's medicinal intrigue.

The antibacterial and antifungal findings suggest that Aquilegia does have an effect in clearing sore throats caused by bacterial infections or oral thrush. This aligns with traditional uses of the plant in various folk medicines for treating throat ailments. Once again, modern science is slowly catching up with what traditional healers have known for centuries.

Personal experience

Of all the flowers in my garden, it's Columbine that I look forward to the most. She's often the first to show her face after winter, her little rosettes of leaves pushing through the soil as soon as February arrives, defying the last frost with a quiet determination. It's always a race between her and my Monkshood, and watching them emerge never fails to make me smile. There's something reassuring about her timing, like an old friend who always turns up just when you need her, and believe me, after January in Wales you need to see a friend.

She grows wild around my house, scattered by the wind and the birds, but I still love planting her, tucking her into the soil with intention. She settles in so easily, as if she's always meant to be there, and once she takes root, she flourishes. She's not fussy, not demanding; she asks for so little yet gives so much in return. She's a friendly presence in the garden, the kind of plant that never seems to stand alone. She thrives in community, popping up in clusters, weaving herself into the landscape, mingling with whatever grows beside her. There's a lesson in that, one of connection, of belonging, of the quiet strength found in supporting those around you.

Columbine teaches the power of voice, of speaking with care, with kindness, with purpose. She whispers that words shape the world around us, that speaking poorly of others doesn't just harm them, it changes the way they see themselves. Words can build or break, lift or crush, and choosing them wisely is an act of responsibility. She reminds me that gossip, cruelty, and careless talk can spread like weeds, strangling what could have been beautiful. In contrast, encouragement, kindness, and simple compliments are like seeds: small, easy to overlook, but capable of growing into something far greater than we ever imagined.

She speaks of small communities, of the impact we have when we work together rather than tearing each other down. It's not about grand gestures, but about the little things, the thoughtful word, the quiet support, the unseen moments that shape the fabric of our shared lives. She asks us to stop focusing on what others are doing wrong and instead look at ourselves, honestly and without excuses. How do we move in the spaces we inhabit? How do we contribute to the world around us? Are we lifting, or are we dragging?

And most importantly, she reminds us that community isn't just about people. It's everything that shares the space where we live—the animals, the plants, the trees, the unseen roots beneath our feet and the wind that carries whispers through the leaves. We are part of something vast, interwoven, inseparable. Columbine is a small flower, delicate in appearance, but she carries deep wisdom. She teaches us that no act of kindness is too small, no effort to support others is wasted, and that true strength lies in knowing we are all connected.

The name that I received from her was Aryr.

Meditation

She is young and willowy, wrapped in a gown of green and purple that shifts like dappled light through the trees. Her hair is wild, tumbling around her shoulders like wind through meadow grass. It makes me smile; I had expected a grandmother in a bonnet, but she is nothing of the sort. That will teach me not to put her in a box.

When she speaks, her voice rings out like tiny silver bells, a tinkling melody that shivers through the air. Her gaze is deep, searching, as if she is not just looking at me but into me. As she talks, she sways gently, like a mother rocking a child, the movement soothing, rhythmic, full of quiet understanding. Her hands dance as she speaks, fingers long and fluid, shaping the space around her. She smiles, and the joy she carries radiates outward, soaking into the warmth of the sun.

The energy she weaves gathers at my throat, a subtle hum at first, but with every word, it grows and unfurls, opening me, urging me to speak, to let my voice flow into the world. It is as though she is inviting me to cast a spell of kindness, of truth, of good things whispered into existence.

She speaks of togetherness, of how we are nothing alone, of how true strength is found in caring for one another. Love of family, yes, but more than that—love of community, of the unbreakable bonds between all living things. She gestures toward the bees, their tireless dance, their devotion to the whole rather than the self. And as if summoned by her words, they come, buzzing between us, golden and glinting in the light, their presence a quiet affirmation of her wisdom.

"All that you need already exists", she says. "The world provides; we only need to remember each other as we live, and it will always be there".

Personal sigil   Kamea sigil

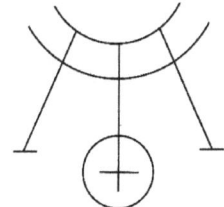 

Aryr

    Hold fast to those around you
    Use your voice to raise them up
    All around you is your family
    They may not look like you
    The music that you weave will be wonderful to hear
    When all support each other and all give what they can
    Raise up the people to the sun
    And let them bring you joy
    For in creating beauty for your loved ones in the world
    The world becomes more wonderful for all that live within

CONCLUSION

As I bring this new version of my book to a close, I cannot ignore the dark tide rising around us. Fascism is surging across the world, creeping into governments, into policies, into the very fabric of our daily lives. If we do not rise to meet it, if we do not take a stand, we risk more than the erosion of our right to walk the Green Path; we risk the silencing of voices, the erasure of freedoms, and the destruction of the sacred balance that binds us to this earth. The people, the plants, the ocean creatures, the rainforest dwellers, all stand on the precipice of devastation, threatened by the unchecked greed of capitalism and the suffocating grip of authoritarian rule. Now, more than ever, we must come together as a community, as kin to all life, and fight for a future where nature is not just protected but revered, where we refuse to let ruthless power sweep away all ecological and spiritual frameworks that hold the world in balance.

At the start of this book, I spoke of an act of quiet revolution, of learning to see the world differently, not through the narrow lens of what we have been taught, nor by the expectations placed upon us, but through the wilder, deeper truth that has always been there, waiting. Now, as we reach the end, I ask you to take one last leap. Step beyond the familiar, out into the living, breathing world, and rekindle your relationship with the Green. Seek out Nature, not as an abstract idea, not as something separate from you, but as something you have always belonged to.

Reconnect. Remember.

For this is not just a call to awaken to the plants, to the trees, to the soil beneath your feet, though their survival is bound to ours. It is a call to act, not just for the sake of the earth but for ourselves. We cannot continue as we are. We stand at a precipice, teetering, choosing to ignore the cracks forming beneath us, pretending that we can take without limit, that we can consume without consequence. But we cannot live like this forever. Our thinking, our doing—both must change.

The earth, the plants, and the creatures will go on, with or without us. Perhaps in a different form, perhaps altered, but they will endure. It is we who are at risk. We who will vanish into memory, fading like breath on glass. And with us, all the things that make us beautiful—our love, our music, our poetry, our dance, our stories, our wild and wondrous selves—lost, dissolved into the past. Unless we change. Unless we rise and make a difference. But we must act now. We must let go of this illusion that we can endlessly take and never give back. We must be willing to make hard choices, to step away from convenience, to ask uncomfortable questions. Do we truly need what we consume so thoughtlessly? Do we need to fly across the world for a fleeting escape? Do we need to own more than we can ever truly use? Can we learn to live with less and find that, in doing so, we have gained more? Can we change the way we grow our food, the way we treat the beings we share this land with, the way we look at the sacred forests, the rivers, the oceans, and see them not as resources to be plundered but as living, breathing kin?

Our world is shaped by the choices we make each day. Every action, every decision, every refusal to question the way things are has brought us here. But that means we also have the power to change our course, to turn away from destruction and towards something whole, something true.

In the end, we owe it to ourselves to stand in awe of the Green, to honour its magnificence, and to remember, truly remember, who we are and why we are here.

To live in community, knowing that every being around us has the right to exist as People. To take only what we need, when we need it, and to understand that "enough" is not a weakness but a wisdom.

To tread upon this earth in reverence, knowing that she is not just land beneath our feet, but a mother who has held us since the dawn of time.

To wake up to the truth that this fierce, fragile, irreplaceable world is the only home we will ever have.

Not them and us but WE.

>Since the mountains became molecules
>And water H2O
>Since our food became a group
>From the temple of Tesco
>Since we gave the Earth just one day
>Instead of every one
>As we battle with each other
>Over every single crumb
>Since we decided we were first not one amongst the many
>and we worked like slaves for masters who grasp at every penny
>Our existence has been fated
>As the magic dissipated
>With the memories of fungi and the road to godhood lost
>Till we see nature in its true form And not as a resource
>When the steward is the servant
>And knows that we are not the first
>We will wander disconnected
>From the forests to the sea
>Til the world goes on without us
>And only memory remains
>Of self-destructive monkeys
>With clever little brains
>And our motorways regreen and our houses overgrow
>And Mother Nature takes a breath, and onward she will go.
>But if we can change our focus
>Away from us and onto we
>We could go on together
>Making life so heavenly
>If we respect the other
>The rocks, the plants, the trees.
>And think of us together
>Not them and us but WE.

BIBLIOGRAPHY

Charubel. *Psychology of Botany: A Treatise on Trees, Shrubs, and Plants, Etc., for the Cure of Diseases and Ailments of the Human System, without Medicine, by Sympathy, Positive and Negative, on the Soul Plane.* Leigh: R. Welch, 1906. https://archive.org/details/PsychologyOfBotany.

Cossins, Dan. "Plant Talk." *The Scientist* 28, no. 1 (2014): 32–7. https://www.the-scientist.com/plant-talk-38209.

Culpeper, Nicholas. *The Complete Herbal.* anboco, 2016.

Dyshlyuk, Lyubov S., Anastasia M. Fedorova, Vyacheslav F. Dolganyuk, and Alexander Yu Prosekov. "Optimization of Extraction of Polyphenolic Compounds from Medicinal Lungwort (Pulmonaria Officinalis L.)." *Journal of Pharmaceutical Research International* 32, no. 24 (2020): 36–45.

Etkin, Nina L. "Ethnopharmocology: Biobehavioral Approaches in the Anthropological Study of Indigenous Medicines." *Annual Review of Anthropology* 17 (1988): 23–42. http://www.jstor.org/stable/2155904.

Junius, Manfred M. *The Practical Handbook of Plant Alchemy: An Herbalist's Guide to Preparing Medicinal Essences, Tinctures, and Elixirs.* Rochester, VT: Inner Traditions, 1985. https://www.simonandschuster.com/books/Spagyrics/Manfred-M-Junius/9781594771798.

Leffler, C. T., S. G. Schwartz, B. Davenport, J. Randolph, J. Busscher, and T. Hadi. "Enduring Influence of Elizabethan Ophthalmic Texts of the 1580s: Bailey, Grassus, and Guillemeau." [In eng]. *Open Ophthalmol J* 8 (2014): 12–8. https://doi.org/10.2174/1874364101408010012.

Leporatti, Maria Laura, and Svetlana Ivancheva. "Traditional Phytotherapy of the Villagers in the Middle Valnerina (Umbria, Central Italy)." *Journal of Ethnopharmacology* 87, nos. 2–3 (2003): 123–35.

Luna, Luis Eduardo. "The Concept of Plants as Teachers among Four Mestizo Shamans of Iquitos, Northeastern Peru." *Journal of ethnopharmacology* 11, no. 2 (1984): 135–56.

Mancuso, Stefano, and Alessandra Viola. *Brilliant Green: The Surprising History and Science of Plant Intelligence*. Island Press, 2015.

Monica Gagliano, PhD. *Thus Spoke the Plant*, United States of America: North Atlantic Books, 2018.

Paduch, Roman, Anna Woźniak, Piotr Niedziela, and Robert Rejdak. "Assessment of Eyebright (Euphrasia Officinalis L.) Extract Activity in Relation to Human Corneal Cells Using in Vitro Tests." [In en]. *Balkan Medical Journal* 2014, no. 1 (January 2014): 29–36. https://doi.org/10.5152/balkanmedj.2014.8377.

Plumwood, Val. "Gender,Eco-Feminism and the Environment." Chap. 3 In *Controversies in Environmental Sociology.*, edited by Rob White, 43–61. United States of America: Cambridge University Press, 2004.

Pratchett, Terry. *Hogfather*. London: Victor Gollancz, 1996. https://www.goodreads.com/quotes/66591.

Tobyn, Graeme. "Dr Reason and Dr Experience: Culpeper's Assignation of Planetary Rulers in the English Physitian." In *From Masha'allah to Kepler: Theory and Practice in Medieval and Renaissance Astrology*, edited by Charles Burnett and Dorian Greenbaum, 473–90. Lampeter: Sophia Centre Press, 2015.

Tupper, Kenneth W. "Entheogens and Existential Intelligence: The Use of Plant Teachers as Cognitive Tools." *Canadian Journal of Education / Revue canadienne de l'éducation* 27, no. 4 (2002): 499–516. https://doi.org/10.2307/1602247. http://www.jstor.org/stable/1602247.

White, Lynn. "The Historical Roots of Our Ecologic Crisis." *Science* 155, no. 3767 (1967): 1203–07. http://www.jstor.org/stable/1720120.

www.ingramcontent.com/pod-product-compliance
Lightning Source LLC
Chambersburg PA
CBHW050904160426
43194CB00011B/2276